EMDR Therapy for Beginners

A Simple Guide to Healing Trauma, Anxiety, and
Negative Memories Without Years of Talk Therapy

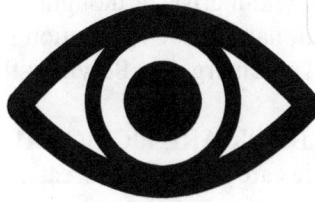

Your First Guide to Eye Movement Therapy for
Trauma and Anxiety Relief

Carolina Pauline Jordan

ISBN: 978-1-7643835-9-2

First Edition: November, 2025

This book provides educational information about ALWAYS seek help from qualified, licensed mental health professionals for trauma, PTSD, anxiety, depression, or any mental health condition. DO NOT attempt EMDR techniques on yourself or others based on this book. Self-treatment may cause psychological harm, retraumatization, or worsening symptoms.

If experiencing a mental health crisis or thoughts of suicide or self-harm, immediately contact National Suicide Prevention Lifeline: 988, Crisis Text Line: HOME to 741741, or Emergency Services: 911.

ALL NAMES IN THIS BOOK ARE FICTIONAL. All personal stories, case studies, and examples are composites created for educational purposes based on common therapeutic scenarios and research literature. They do not represent actual individuals or real cases. Any resemblance to actual persons, living or deceased, is purely coincidental. Names including Marcus, Jennifer, Tyler, Patricia, David, Rita, Kevin, Maya, Diego, Antonio, Carlos, Kayla, Isaiah, Amara, Garrett, Hannah, Bethany, Cameron, Nicole, Trevor, Vanessa, Brandon, Diana, Oscar, Gina, Frank, Lily, Patrick, Dana, Elena, Jamal, Carmen, Anthony, Isabella, Nina, Gregory, Veronica, Olivia, and all others are fictional. No confidential therapeutic information has been disclosed.

Information is based on published research and established EMDR protocols. This book claims no affiliation with EMDR Institute, EMDRIA, or other professional organizations unless explicitly stated. Individual results vary significantly based on trauma severity, therapist expertise, client readiness, and many other factors. Success stories represent possible results, not guarantees. Some individuals may not respond to EMDR therapy or may experience temporary symptom increases.

By reading this book, you acknowledge: this book is educational, not therapeutic; you will not use it as substitute for professional care; you will seek qualified professional help; you accept full responsibility for your mental health decisions; you release the author and publisher from liability.

Table of Contents

CHAPTER 1: What is EMDR Therapy?...1

What Makes EMDR Different? 1

The Talk Therapy vs. EMDR Difference 2

How Fast Does EMDR Work? 3

The Science of Stuck Memories 4

What EMDR Does to "Unstick" Memories 5

The Memory Doesn't Disappear 5

A Different Kind of Healing 6

Who Can Benefit from EMDR?.....................................7

What EMDR Cannot Fix..8

Key Takaway..8

CHAPTER 2: How Does EMDR Actually Work? 10

Your Brain's Natural Healing System 10

When the System Gets Blocked...............................11

The Eye Movement Connection................................12

What Happens During Processing 12

The Working Memory Theory 13

Why Not Just Eye Movements Alone? 14

The Train Track Analogy 15

The Digestive System Comparison...........................16

Different Types of Bilateral Stimulation..................17

Why Some Memories Get Stuck and Others Don't..............18

The Reconnection Process 19

CHAPTER 3: What Can EMDR Help With? 21

Post-Traumatic Stress Disorder (PTSD): EMDR's Main Application 21

Anxiety Disorders: When Fear Takes Over 23

Depression: When Sadness Won't Lift 25

Specific Phobias: Fear That Doesn't Make Sense 26

Grief and Loss: When Mourning Gets Stuck 28

Performance Anxiety: Fear of Failure 28

Low Self-Esteem and Negative Self-Beliefs 29

What EMDR Cannot Fix 30

How Do You Know If EMDR Might Help You? 31

EMDR's Growing Applications 32

CHAPTER 4: The 8 Phases of EMDR Therapy **33**

Phase 1: History Taking and Treatment Planning 33

Phase 2: Preparation 34

Phase 3: Assessment 36

Phase 4: Desensitization 39

Phase 5: Installation 42

Phase 6: Body Scan 43

Phase 7: Closure 44

Phase 8: Re-evaluation 46

What Makes EMDR Different from Other Therapies 47

Key Takeaways 48

CHAPTER 5: What to Expect: Your First EMDR Session and Beyond
.... **49**

Finding a Qualified EMDR Therapist ..: 49

Questions to Ask During Your Consultation 51

Your First Session: What Actually Happens 52

The Preparation Session: Building Your Toolkit......................55

Your First Processing Session: The Real Deal 57

Between Sessions: What to Expect 61

How Long Does EMDR Take? 63

What Sessions Actually Cost 64

In-Person vs. Online EMDR 65

After EMDR: Maintaining Your Progress................................67

The Bottom Line 68

CHAPTER 6: Real Stories of Transformation: EMDR Success Cases
..70

Story 1: Marcus - Combat Veteran with PTSD 70

Story 2: Jennifer - Sexual Assault Survivor 72

Story 3: Tyler - Childhood Abuse and Low Self-Esteem.........75

Story 4: Patricia - Phobia of Driving After an Accident 77

Story 5: David - Performance Anxiety and Past Humiliation..80

Story 6: Rita - Complicated Grief After Losing Her Son.........82

What These Stories Teach Us..85

CHAPTER 7: Common Myths About EMDR 87

"Will EMDR make me relive my trauma?" 87

"Is EMDR hypnosis?" 88

"Will EMDR erase my memories?" 89

"What if I cry or get really upset during a session?"...............90

"Can EMDR make things worse?"..91

"Do the eye movements really matter, or is EMDR just
exposure therapy?"..92

"Is EMDR scientifically proven?" 93

"How is EMDR different from regular therapy?"....................94

"Can I do EMDR on myself?" 95

"What if I can't remember the traumatic event clearly?" 96

"Will my therapist judge me for what I reveal?".....................97

"Can EMDR help with [specific condition]?" 97

"How long do the results last?" 98

"What if EMDR doesn't work for me?" 99

Key Take always on Concerns and Myths 100

CHAPTER 8: Your EMDR Action Plan **101**

Is EMDR Right for You? A Self-Assessment.......................101

Finding an EMDR Therapist: Your Step-by-Step Guide 103

Preparing for Your First Appointment....................................106

Supporting Your EMDR Journey 108

What to Do After EMDR 110

Resources 111

Your Action Plan: Next Steps..112

A Final Word 113

References...**115**

AUTHOR'S NOTE

This book was written to make information about EMDR therapy accessible to people who are suffering and seeking help. I have compiled and synthesized research, clinical literature, and established therapeutic protocols to create an educational resource for those considering EMDR treatment.

My goal is to demystify EMDR therapy, explain how it works in plain language, and help readers make informed decisions about their mental health care. This book is meant to be a starting point, a guide that helps you understand what EMDR is and if it might be right for you.

However, understanding EMDR and receiving EMDR therapy are two different things. I strongly encourage anyone dealing with trauma, PTSD, anxiety, or other mental health concerns to work with qualified, licensed mental health professionals who have completed proper EMDR training.

If this book helps even one person find the courage to seek help and begin their healing journey, it will have served its purpose.

Be kind to yourself. Healing is possible.

Carolina Pauline Jordan

Researcher and Mental Health Professional

CHAPTER 1: What is EMDR Therapy?

Imagine this: It's 1987, and a psychologist named Dr. Francine Shapiro is taking a walk through a park in California. She's dealing with some disturbing thoughts that have been bothering her. As she walks, she notices something strange happening. Her eyes are moving back and forth naturally, following the scenery around her, and somehow, those upsetting thoughts are becoming less intense.

Most people would have brushed this off as a coincidence. But Dr. Shapiro was curious. She started experimenting deliberately moving her eyes from side to side while thinking about things that upset her. The same thing happened. The emotional charge of those memories seemed to decrease. She began testing this with other people, and they reported similar results.

That accidental discovery in a park became what we now know as EMDR therapy, which stands for Eye Movement Desensitization and Reprocessing. Today, it's one of the most effective treatments for trauma and many other mental health issues. Organizations like the World Health Organization, the U.S. Department of Veterans Affairs, and mental health associations worldwide recommend it as a proven treatment.

What Makes EMDR Different?

Let's start with what EMDR is *not*. It's not traditional talk therapy where you sit on a couch for years discussing your childhood. It's not hypnosis where someone puts you in a trance. And it's not about forgetting your past or pretending bad things never happened.

Here's what EMDR actually is: It's a way to help your brain process difficult memories so they stop causing problems in your present life.

Think about it this way. When you cut your finger, your body knows exactly what to do. It sends healing cells to the wound, forms a scab, and eventually, the cut heals. You might have a small scar, but it doesn't hurt anymore. Your body has a natural healing process.

Your brain has a similar system for processing experiences. When something happens to you—good or bad—your brain is supposed to take that experience, process it, learn from it, and file it away as a memory. The memory stays, but it shouldn't keep causing you pain.

But sometimes, when something really terrible happens—a car crash, an assault, abuse, a devastating loss—it's like that mental "wound" gets infected. Your brain's natural healing process gets blocked. The memory doesn't get properly processed and stored. Instead, it stays "active" in your brain, causing ongoing problems.

The Talk Therapy vs. EMDR Difference

Let me introduce you to Kevin. At 24, he was in a serious motorcycle accident. He survived with minor physical injuries, but mentally, he was a wreck. Every time he heard a loud noise, he'd freeze up. He couldn't ride his motorcycle anymore. Even riding in cars made him anxious. He'd have nightmares about the crash several times a week.

Kevin tried traditional counseling. He spent months talking about the accident, discussing his feelings, exploring why he felt the way he did. His therapist was great, and talking did help him understand his reactions better. But after six months, he still jumped at loud noises. He still had the nightmares. Understanding why he felt anxious didn't make the anxiety go away.

Then Kevin tried EMDR. In his first session, his therapist explained that they wouldn't need to discuss every detail of the accident over and over. Instead, they'd help his brain reprocess the memory of the crash. After just eight EMDR sessions spread over two months, Kevin's nightmares stopped. He could hear loud noises without panicking. He wasn't "cured" of all anxiety, but the crash no longer controlled his life.

What's the difference? Traditional therapy often works by helping you understand your problems and develop coping strategies. That's valuable, and for many issues, it works great. But with trauma, sometimes understanding why you feel bad doesn't make you feel better. The traumatic memory is still stored in your brain in a way that keeps triggering distress.

EMDR works directly with how that memory is stored. It helps your brain reprocess the memory so it becomes "just" a memory— something that happened in the past—rather than something that feels like it's still happening now.

How Fast Does EMDR Work?

This is one of the most surprising things about EMDR. While traditional therapy for trauma might take years, EMDR often produces results much faster.

Let me tell you about Maya. She'd been dealing with the effects of childhood neglect for 15 years. She'd been in and out of therapy since college, trying different approaches. Some helped a little. Some didn't help at all. When she started EMDR at age 32, she was skeptical. She'd tried so many things before.

Her therapist told her that for a single traumatic event, EMDR usually takes 3-6 sessions. For complex trauma like Maya's— multiple traumatic experiences over time—it might take 12-20 sessions. That still sounds like a lot, but compared to the 15 years she'd already been struggling, it was nothing.

Maya processed her first target memory in her fourth EMDR session. She worked on a specific memory of being left alone as a child. During the processing, she cried, felt angry, and experienced a range of emotions. But by the end of that session, when she thought about that memory, the crushing sadness she'd always felt was gone. The memory was still there. She could still recall it. But it didn't hurt anymore.

She continued EMDR for several months, working through different memories. Within six months, Maya felt better than she had in her entire adult life. The depression that had shadowed her for years lifted. She stopped having panic attacks. Her relationships improved because she wasn't reacting to everything through the lens of her childhood trauma.

The Science of Stuck Memories

Let's get a bit more specific about what happens in your brain when memories get stuck.

Your brain has an information processing system. Think of it like a sophisticated filing system. Every day, your brain takes in thousands of experiences—sights, sounds, smells, emotions, thoughts, physical sensations. Most of these get processed automatically while you sleep. Your brain files them away appropriately, learns from them, and moves on.

For example, let's say you're learning to cook and you burn yourself on a hot pan. Your brain processes this experience: touching hot pans = pain. Lesson learned. The next time you're near a hot pan, you're cautious, but you're not traumatized. The memory is filed away as "useful information" rather than as an ongoing threat.

But trauma is different. When something overwhelmingly bad happens, especially if it happens suddenly or you feel helpless, your brain's processing system can get overloaded. It's like trying to save a file on a computer during a power surge—the file gets corrupted.

The traumatic memory doesn't get properly processed and filed away. Instead, it stays in your brain in its raw, unprocessed form. And because it's not properly stored as a "past event," your brain treats it like it's still happening. That's why people with trauma often say things like, "I know it was years ago, but it feels like yesterday."

Marcus experienced this firsthand. He was robbed at gunpoint when he was 19. The actual robbery lasted maybe three minutes. But ten years later, at age 29, he was still having problems. He couldn't go to the convenience store where it happened. He felt anxious in parking lots. When someone walked up behind him unexpectedly, his heart would race.

Marcus knew logically that he was safe. He knew the robbery was over. But his brain didn't know that. The memory was stuck, unprocessed, and his brain kept treating that three-minute event as if it was an ongoing threat.

What EMDR Does to "Unstick" Memories

Here's where EMDR comes in. The therapy uses bilateral stimulation—usually side-to-side eye movements—while you briefly focus on the traumatic memory. This bilateral stimulation seems to activate your brain's natural processing system, the same one that processes memories during REM sleep (when your eyes move back and forth naturally).

When Marcus did EMDR, his therapist asked him to think about the robbery while following her finger moving back and forth across his field of vision. This sounds weird, I know. Marcus thought it sounded ridiculous at first. But here's what happened:

As he moved his eyes back and forth while thinking about the robbery, his brain started processing the memory. New insights emerged. He remembered things he'd forgotten—like the fact that he had survived, that he'd handled the situation, that the robber was probably more scared than he was. The intense fear began to decrease. His body started to relax.

After several sets of eye movements, when Marcus thought about the robbery, it felt different. The memory was still there—he could still recall what happened—but the emotional intensity was gone. It felt like something that happened in the past, not something happening now.

The Memory Doesn't Disappear

This is important to understand: EMDR doesn't erase your memories. Some people worry about this. "What if I forget important parts of my life?" they ask.

Let me introduce you to Rachel. Her father died when she was 16 in a car accident. The grief was crushing. But mixed with the grief was trauma—she'd been the one to identify his body at the hospital, an image that haunted her for years. She couldn't think about her father without immediately seeing that image and feeling overwhelmed.

When Rachel considered EMDR at age 28, she worried: "What if EMDR makes me forget my dad? What if I lose the good memories too?"

Her therapist explained that EMDR doesn't delete memories. It doesn't make you forget. What it does is change how the memory is stored in your brain and how your brain reacts to it.

After EMDR, Rachel could still remember everything about her father. She remembered his laugh, his terrible jokes, the way he made pancakes on Sunday mornings. She also remembered the accident and seeing him at the hospital. But that traumatic image was no longer the first thing her brain went to when she thought of him. The good memories became accessible again. The traumatic memory was still there, but it had been reprocessed and properly stored as a past event.

She could think about her father and feel sadness—grief is natural and appropriate—but not that overwhelming, crushing pain that made it impossible to remember him at all.

A Different Kind of Healing

Traditional therapy often works through insight and understanding. EMDR works differently. It's more like physical therapy for your brain.

When Jamal broke his arm playing basketball at age 22, he needed physical therapy afterward. The physical therapist didn't just talk to him about his arm. She didn't just help him understand what happened to the bones and muscles. She guided him through specific exercises that helped his arm heal and regain strength.

EMDR is similar. Your therapist guides you through specific procedures that help your brain process traumatic memories. You're not just talking about what happened. You're actually processing it in a way that leads to healing.

Jamal, coincidentally, also ended up needing EMDR later. He developed intense anxiety after witnessing a shooting in his neighborhood. Talk therapy helped him understand his anxiety, but EMDR helped resolve it. Just like physical therapy had helped his arm heal, EMDR helped his brain process what he'd witnessed.

Who Can Benefit from EMDR?

EMDR was originally developed for post-traumatic stress disorder (PTSD), and that's still what it's best known for. Veterans, assault survivors, accident victims, abuse survivors—EMDR has helped millions of people with trauma.

But here's what researchers discovered: EMDR helps with a lot more than just PTSD. It can help with anxiety, depression, phobias, grief, and many other issues—as long as those issues are rooted in past negative experiences.

Think about Elena. She had terrible public speaking anxiety. Standing in front of people made her feel physically ill. Through EMDR, she and her therapist traced this back to being humiliated by a teacher in front of her class when she was 12. She'd given a presentation and mispronounced several words. The teacher had mocked her in front of everyone. The other kids laughed.

Elena had forgotten about this incident for years. It was just one bad day in middle school. But her brain had stored that experience in a way that continued to affect her 15 years later. Every time she had to speak in front of people, her brain was essentially saying, "Warning! This situation led to humiliation before. Danger!"

After processing that middle school memory with EMDR, Elena's public speaking anxiety dramatically decreased. The humiliating memory was still there, but it no longer controlled her present-day reactions.

What EMDR Cannot Fix

It's important to be realistic about what EMDR can and cannot do. EMDR works on problems rooted in how memories are stored and processed. If your mental health issue stems from something else—a chemical imbalance, a genetic condition, a brain injury, or a current ongoing stressful situation—EMDR might not be the right treatment.

For instance, if someone has depression that runs in their family and has been present since childhood with no clear traumatic cause, EMDR probably won't fix it. If someone has bipolar disorder, EMDR won't treat the bipolar disorder itself (though it might help with trauma that person experienced).

Also, EMDR works on past events, not current ones. If you're in an ongoing abusive relationship, EMDR can't fix that. You need to get to safety first. If you're experiencing current, ongoing stress—like going through a divorce or dealing with a serious illness—those are present problems, not past traumatic memories. EMDR might be helpful later, after the situation is resolved, but it's not a tool for dealing with current crises.

Key Takaway

EMDR is a proven therapy that helps your brain process traumatic and distressing memories so they stop causing problems in your present life. It works faster than traditional talk therapy for many people. It doesn't require you to discuss every detail of your trauma. It doesn't erase memories. And it helps with more than just PTSD.

Think of EMDR as removing a splinter. The splinter (the unprocessed traumatic memory) has been causing pain and inflammation. You've been putting bandages on it, taking pain medication, trying to ignore it. But it keeps hurting. EMDR removes the splinter so your brain can heal naturally.

In the next chapter, we'll look more closely at how EMDR actually works—what's happening in your brain during those eye movements, and why this seemingly strange process produces such powerful results.

CHAPTER 2: How Does EMDR Actually Work?

If you told someone 50 years ago that moving your eyes back and forth while thinking about trauma could heal psychological wounds, they'd probably think you were crazy. Even today, when people first hear about EMDR, a common reaction is: "That sounds too simple to work."

But it does work. Study after study has confirmed it. The question is: how?

Your Brain's Natural Healing System

Let's start with what happens in your brain under normal circumstances.

Every night while you sleep, your brain does something fascinating. During REM sleep (Rapid Eye Movement sleep—yes, the same eye movement thing), your brain processes the day's experiences. It sorts through everything that happened, decides what's important, what can be forgotten, files memories away appropriately, and makes connections between new and old information.

Think of it like your brain doing overnight maintenance, like how your computer runs updates while you're not using it.

Miguel, a biology student, experienced this firsthand when studying for his organic chemistry exam. He'd spent all day trying to understand a complicated concept about molecular bonds. He went to bed frustrated, feeling like he'd never get it. But when he woke up the next morning and looked at his notes, suddenly it made sense. His brain had processed the information overnight.

This same overnight processing system handles emotional experiences too. Let's say you have an argument with your best friend. You go to bed upset. But after a good night's sleep, you often wake up with a clearer perspective. The situation hasn't changed, but your brain has processed your emotional reaction to it. You can think more clearly about what happened and what to do next.

This is your brain's adaptive information processing system at work. It's constantly taking raw experiences and emotions, processing them, learning from them, and integrating them into your broader life experience.

When the System Gets Blocked

But trauma can overwhelm this system. When something terrible happens—something that triggers intense fear, helplessness, or horror—your brain gets flooded with stress hormones. Your fight-or-flight system goes into overdrive. And in that state, your brain's normal processing system doesn't work properly.

The traumatic memory gets stored, but it's stored wrong. Instead of being processed and filed away as a past event, it stays in your brain in its raw, unprocessed form, complete with all the intense emotions, physical sensations, and distorted beliefs from the moment of trauma.

Let me tell you about Diana. She was attacked by a dog when she was eight years old while walking to school. The dog came out of nowhere, knocked her down, and bit her arm. The attack lasted maybe 30 seconds before the dog's owner pulled it away. Diana needed stitches but otherwise recovered fine.

Or so everyone thought.

Twenty years later, at age 28, Diana still couldn't walk past dogs without her heart racing. She crossed the street to avoid them. She turned down invitations to friends' houses if they had dogs. She knew most dogs were friendly. She knew logically that one bad experience 20 years ago didn't mean all dogs were dangerous. But knowledge didn't change how she felt.

What happened? That 30-second attack got stored in Diana's brain in an unprocessed state. The memory was stuck with all the terror of that moment intact. And because it wasn't properly processed as a past event, her brain treated every dog as a current threat. Her brain was essentially frozen in that moment, saying, "Dog = danger! Dog = danger!" over and over, despite 20 years of evidence to the contrary.

The Eye Movement Connection

So how do eye movements help? This is where it gets interesting, and I'll be honest—scientists are still figuring out exactly why it works. But here's what we know.

Remember REM sleep, when your eyes move rapidly back and forth while your brain processes memories? EMDR seems to activate that same processing system, but while you're awake.

When you move your eyes back and forth (or experience other forms of bilateral stimulation like tapping alternately on your left and right hands), it appears to stimulate both hemispheres of your brain. This bilateral stimulation seems to help your brain access the stuck traumatic memory and reprocess it the way it should have been processed originally.

Think of it this way: The traumatic memory is like a computer file that got corrupted. Your brain keeps trying to open it, but it won't open properly, so you keep getting error messages (anxiety, nightmares, panic, etc.). EMDR is like running a repair program that fixes the corrupted file so it can be properly accessed, processed, and stored.

What Happens During Processing

Let's walk through what actually happens in your brain during EMDR, using Diego's experience as an example.

Diego was in a serious car accident at age 23. Someone ran a red light and T-boned his car. Diego wasn't badly hurt physically—some bruises and a mild concussion. But the crash left a mark on his brain. He became terrified of driving and even being a passenger in cars. Approaching any intersection made him panic.

During EMDR, Diego's therapist asked him to bring up the memory of the accident while following her finger moving back and forth. At first, thinking about the accident made Diego intensely anxious. His heart raced. His palms sweated. He felt the same terror he'd felt during the crash.

But as he continued the eye movements, something shifted. New thoughts and connections started emerging. He remembered that he'd unbuckled his seatbelt and gotten out of the car himself—he hadn't been helpless. He realized the accident wasn't his fault—the other driver ran the light. He thought about other times he'd driven safely, thousands of times without incident.

These weren't things his therapist told him. They were connections his own brain was making as the memory got reprocessed. With each set of eye movements, the emotional intensity decreased a bit more. The physical sensations of panic subsided. The memory started feeling less immediate, less overwhelming.

By the end of the session, Diego could think about the accident without panicking. The memory was still there—he could recall what happened—but it felt like something that happened in the past, not something happening right now.

The Working Memory Theory

One of the leading theories about why EMDR works is called the working memory theory. Working memory is your brain's ability to hold and process information in the moment. It's like your brain's RAM (random access memory).

When you're doing something that takes up working memory—like following a moving finger with your eyes—you have less working memory available for other things. So when you're thinking about a traumatic memory while also doing eye movements, you can't fully engage with that memory in the intense, overwhelming way you normally would.

This might sound bad—don't we want to fully process the memory? But here's the key: By preventing you from fully re-experiencing the trauma, the eye movements allow you to access the memory and process it without becoming completely overwhelmed by it. You can think about it from a slight distance, which allows your brain to integrate new, more adaptive information.

Think of it like this: Normally, when someone with trauma thinks about their traumatic memory, it's like being sucked into a whirlpool. The memory pulls them completely into that moment, with all its terror and pain. They're drowning in it.

During EMDR, the eye movements are like holding onto a rope while you look into the whirlpool. You can see it, you can examine it, but you're not being pulled under. You maintain enough distance to process what you're seeing without being overwhelmed by it.

Why Not Just Eye Movements Alone?

Some people have wondered: If eye movements help process memories, why not just move your eyes back and forth on your own? Why do you need a therapist and all these phases of treatment?

Great question. Let me tell you what happened to Patrick when he tried this.

Patrick read about EMDR online. He had some traumatic memories from his time in the military that bothered him. He figured he'd save money and try the eye movement thing himself. He sat in his room, thought about a traumatic memory, and moved his eyes back and forth.

At first, he felt a bit better. But then the memory became more intense. He started feeling overwhelmed. His heart raced. He began having a panic attack. He had to stop, and he felt worse than before he started.

What went wrong? EMDR isn't just eye movements. It's a complete, eight-phase treatment protocol that includes:

- Preparation and stabilization
- Identifying the right target memories
- Establishing resources and coping skills
- Proper setup and assessment of the memory
- The actual reprocessing with bilateral stimulation
- Installation of positive beliefs
- Checking that the processing is complete
- Follow-up to ensure lasting change

The eye movements are just one part of a carefully structured process. A trained therapist knows how to guide you through this process safely, how to help when you get stuck, and how to ensure you're truly processing the memory rather than just re-traumatizing yourself.

The Train Track Analogy

My favorite way to explain EMDR is the train track analogy. Imagine your memories are trains running on tracks through your brain. Most of your memories run smoothly from station to station. You can access them when you need to, they provide useful information, and they don't cause problems.

But traumatic memories are like trains that have derailed. They're stuck off the tracks, blocking everything up, causing problems. Every time your brain tries to route new experiences through that area, it hits this derailed train and has to deal with all the wreckage.

EMDR helps get that train back on the tracks. The train (memory) is still there—you haven't gotten rid of it. But now it can run smoothly through your brain's system without causing a massive pileup every time you encounter something that reminds you of it.

Carmen experienced this with her memory of being bullied in high school. For years, that memory was derailed in her brain. Any social situation that felt even slightly similar—meeting new people, being in a group where she might be judged—would trigger intense anxiety. It was like her brain kept hitting that derailed train of the bullying memory.

After EMDR put that memory back on track (processed it properly), Carmen could still remember being bullied. But when she walked into new social situations, her brain didn't automatically route her through that old trauma anymore. She could evaluate each new situation based on what was actually happening now, not based on what happened 15 years ago.

The Digestive System Comparison

Another helpful way to think about EMDR is to compare it to your digestive system.

When you eat food, your body digests it—breaks it down, extracts the nutrients, and eliminates the waste. This is a natural, automatic process. You don't have to think about it or try to make it happen. Your body just does it.

But sometimes you eat something that your body can't digest properly. Maybe it's spoiled food, or maybe you have a food intolerance. That food sits in your system causing problems—pain, nausea, discomfort. Your body keeps trying to process it but can't.

Traumatic memories are like food your brain can't digest. Your brain keeps trying to process them (you have recurring nightmares, intrusive thoughts, flashbacks) but can't break them down properly.

The memory just sits there in your mental system, causing ongoing pain and discomfort.

EMDR helps your brain digest those memories. The memory gets properly broken down, the useful parts are integrated (lessons learned, awareness of your strength, etc.), and the toxic parts—the overwhelming emotions and distorted beliefs—get eliminated. The memory moves through your system instead of getting stuck.

Different Types of Bilateral Stimulation

While eye movements are the most common form of bilateral stimulation in EMDR, they're not the only option. Your therapist might use:

Alternating tapping: You hold small devices that vibrate alternately in your left and right hands. Or the therapist might tap alternately on your knees or shoulders.

Alternating sounds: You wear headphones that play sounds alternating between your left and right ears.

Alternating visual cues: You might watch lights blinking back and forth instead of following a finger.

All of these provide bilateral stimulation—stimulation that alternates between the left and right sides of your body. They all seem to produce similar effects, though eye movements are considered the most powerful.

When Anthony did EMDR, he had a hard time with the eye movements. Following the therapist's finger made him dizzy. So his therapist switched to the tappers—small devices he held in his hands that buzzed alternately. This worked much better for him. The processing happened just as effectively.

The key isn't the specific method. The key is the bilateral stimulation that seems to activate your brain's processing system.

Why Some Memories Get Stuck and Others Don't

You might wonder: If trauma can block memory processing, why do some traumatic events get processed naturally while others get stuck?

Several factors influence this:

The severity of the trauma: More severe trauma is more likely to overwhelm your processing system.

Your age when it happened: Children's brains are still developing, so trauma in childhood is more likely to get stuck.

Your support system: Having people to help you process the experience afterward makes a big difference.

Previous trauma: If you've had other unprocessed trauma, new trauma is more likely to get stuck.

The element of surprise: Sudden, unexpected trauma is harder to process than something you had time to prepare for.

Feeling helpless: Trauma where you couldn't do anything to protect yourself or others is more likely to stick.

Isabella and Nina were in the same natural disaster—a major earthquake. Both were terrified during the quake. But Isabella had some previous trauma from her childhood that was unprocessed. Nina had a strong support system and no prior trauma. The earthquake shook them both up, but Isabella developed PTSD while Nina, though understandably shaken for a while, didn't. Isabella's prior trauma made her more vulnerable to developing PTSD from the earthquake.

This doesn't mean Nina was stronger or that Isabella was weaker. It means their brains' processing systems were in different states when the earthquake hit.

The Reconnection Process

One more important thing happens during EMDR: Your brain starts making new connections.

Traumatic memories often get stored in isolation, disconnected from other, more adaptive memories. It's like the traumatic memory is locked in a room by itself, cut off from everything else you know.

During EMDR, as the memory gets reprocessed, your brain starts connecting it to other information. You start accessing memories of your own strength and resilience. You start connecting to the fact that the trauma is over, that you survived, that you've handled difficult things since then.

When Garrett processed his memory of a violent mugging, he suddenly remembered other times he'd been in difficult situations and handled them well. He connected the trauma memory to his current life, where he was safe. He linked it to his understanding that what happened wasn't his fault. These connections weren't there before EMDR—the trauma memory was isolated, frozen in time.

Once those connections formed, the trauma memory was integrated into Garrett's broader life story instead of standing alone as this overwhelming, disconnected experience.

The Bottom Line on How It Works

EMDR activates your brain's natural information processing system—the same one that processes memories during REM sleep. Through bilateral stimulation (usually eye movements), EMDR helps your brain access stuck traumatic memories and reprocess them the way they should have been processed originally.

During this reprocessing, several things happen:

- The emotional intensity decreases
- New insights and connections emerge

- The memory gets properly integrated with other information
- Your brain recognizes the trauma as a past event, not a present threat
- Distorted beliefs get updated with more accurate information

The memory doesn't disappear, but it transforms from something that controls you into something that's just part of your history.

In the next chapter, we'll look at all the different issues EMDR can help with—because it turns out that unprocessed memories cause a much wider range of problems than just PTSD.

CHAPTER 3: What Can EMDR Help With?

When Dr. Shapiro first developed EMDR, she focused on treating post-traumatic stress disorder. But as therapists started using EMDR with more people, they made an interesting discovery: It helped with a lot more than just PTSD.

This makes sense when you understand how EMDR works. If the core problem is unprocessed memories causing current symptoms, then EMDR can help with any condition where unprocessed memories are at the root of the problem.

Post-Traumatic Stress Disorder (PTSD): EMDR's Main Application

Let's start with what EMDR is best known for: PTSD.

PTSD develops after experiencing or witnessing a traumatic event. Not everyone who experiences trauma develops PTSD, but for those who do, the symptoms are severe and long-lasting:

- Intrusive memories or flashbacks
- Nightmares about the trauma
- Severe anxiety or panic when reminded of the trauma
- Avoiding anything that reminds you of the trauma
- Negative changes in thinking and mood
- Being easily startled or always on guard

PTSD is more than just feeling upset about something bad that happened. It's your brain getting stuck in survival mode, constantly replaying the trauma, constantly scanning for danger.

Marcus served two tours in Afghanistan with the Marines. He saw combat, lost friends, and lived through experiences that most people couldn't imagine. When he came home at age 26, he thought he'd left the war behind. But the war hadn't left him.

He couldn't sleep without nightmares. Fireworks on the Fourth of July sent him into a panic. He couldn't go to crowded places because he was always scanning for threats. He jumped at unexpected sounds. He felt disconnected from his wife and kids. He started drinking to numb the feelings.

Traditional therapy helped somewhat. He learned about PTSD, developed some coping skills. But the nightmares continued. The hypervigilance continued. He still felt like he was in danger even though he was safe at home in Oregon.

Then Marcus tried EMDR. His therapist asked him to identify his worst memories from Afghanistan—not to talk about them in detail, but just to identify them as targets for processing.

They started with the memory that bothered him most: the day his friend Daniel died in an IED explosion. This memory haunted Marcus. He'd see it in flashbacks. He'd dream about it. Thinking about it made him feel like he was right back there.

During EMDR, as Marcus briefly focused on this memory while doing eye movements, something shifted. At first, the memory was overwhelming—the same terror, guilt, and grief he always felt. But as the processing continued, new perspectives emerged.

He remembered that Daniel had died instantly—he hadn't suffered. He realized he'd done everything possible in that moment. He connected to the fact that he was no longer in Afghanistan—he was in Oregon, safe with his family. He recognized that Daniel wouldn't have wanted Marcus to suffer for the rest of his life.

These weren't things his therapist told him. They were insights his own brain arrived at as the memory got reprocessed.

After six EMDR sessions focusing on different combat memories, Marcus's nightmares became less frequent. After twelve sessions, they were rare. The hypervigilance decreased. He stopped jumping at every unexpected sound. He could enjoy fireworks with his kids. He felt connected to his family again.

The memories of Afghanistan didn't disappear. Marcus could still recall what happened. But those memories no longer controlled his present life. They were in the past, where they belonged.

Anxiety Disorders: When Fear Takes Over

Anxiety disorders are incredibly common. They include generalized anxiety disorder (constant worry), panic disorder (sudden panic attacks), and social anxiety (fear of social situations). EMDR can help with all of these when they're rooted in past experiences.

Generalized Anxiety Disorder (GAD)

People with GAD worry excessively about everything—work, health, money, relationships, the future. The worry is hard to control and interferes with daily life.

Nicole had GAD that started in college and continued for 15 years. She worried constantly. She worried about being late, about making mistakes, about people being angry with her, about her health, about her job security. The worry was exhausting.

Through EMDR, Nicole and her therapist traced this anxiety back to growing up with a parent who was unpredictable and sometimes explosive. Nicole never knew when her mom would blow up over small things. She learned to be constantly vigilant, trying to anticipate and prevent problems.

That survival strategy had made sense when she was a child living in that environment. But Nicole was now 37, living on her own, with a stable job and healthy relationships. The constant vigilance wasn't necessary anymore. But her brain hadn't gotten that message.

EMDR helped Nicole process memories of her mother's angry outbursts. As these memories were reprocessed, her general anxiety level decreased. She could differentiate between her childhood, where vigilance was necessary, and her present life, where it wasn't. The constant worry didn't disappear overnight, but it became manageable in a way it never had been before.

Panic Disorder

Panic attacks are sudden episodes of intense fear that come on quickly and peak within minutes. Your heart races, you can't breathe, you feel like you're dying. Panic disorder is when you have recurring panic attacks and live in fear of having another one.

Trevor started having panic attacks at age 19. They seemed to come out of nowhere. He'd be sitting in class or driving his car, and suddenly his heart would start racing, he couldn't catch his breath, and he'd feel like he was having a heart attack. He went to the emergency room three times before doctors told him he was having panic attacks, not heart attacks.

For five years, Trevor lived in fear of the next panic attack. He started avoiding situations where he'd had attacks before. He couldn't drive on highways. He had trouble sitting through classes. His world kept getting smaller.

In EMDR, Trevor's therapist asked him to think back to when his first panic attack happened. Trevor realized it occurred a week after his best friend from high school died suddenly in a car accident. The funeral was the week before the first panic attack.

They used EMDR to process his grief and trauma around his friend's death. Trevor hadn't recognized this connection before. He thought the panic attacks were random. But as he processed the trauma and grief, the panic attacks became less frequent. Eventually, they stopped.

Trevor's panic attacks were his body's stuck response to a trauma he hadn't fully processed. Once that trauma was addressed, the panic attacks resolved.

Depression: When Sadness Won't Lift

Depression isn't just feeling sad. It's a persistent heaviness that affects your sleep, appetite, energy, concentration, and ability to enjoy things that used to bring pleasure.

Not all depression is caused by unprocessed memories. Some depression is biochemical or genetic. But when depression is linked to past experiences—loss, trauma, abuse, failure—EMDR can help.

Vanessa had been depressed on and off since her early twenties. She was 35 now. Antidepressants helped some, but she still felt a persistent sadness. Therapy had helped her understand herself better, but the depression remained.

In EMDR, Vanessa identified several memories that seemed connected to her depression:

- Being severely bullied in middle school
- Her parents' bitter divorce when she was 15
- A relationship in college where her boyfriend had been emotionally abusive
- Failing out of nursing school, her dream career

These memories carried themes of worthlessness, failure, and being unlovable. Even though these events were years in the past, the negative beliefs from those experiences—"I'm not good enough," "I'm unlovable," "I'm a failure"—continued to color how Vanessa saw herself.

EMDR helped Vanessa process each of these memories. As she reprocessed the bullying, she recognized it wasn't about her—those kids were dealing with their own issues. As she processed her parents' divorce, she realized she wasn't responsible for their relationship problems. Processing the abusive relationship helped her see that his treatment of her reflected his problems, not her worth. And reprocessing her failure in nursing school, she recognized that having to change career paths didn't make her a failure as a person.

As these memories were reprocessed and the negative beliefs were updated, Vanessa's depression lifted. It wasn't instant—it took several months of EMDR. But gradually, that heaviness that had shadowed her for years began to fade.

Specific Phobias: Fear That Doesn't Make Sense

Phobias are intense, irrational fears of specific things—heights, flying, needles, dogs, spiders, blood, enclosed spaces. People with phobias know their fear is out of proportion to the actual danger, but they can't control it.

EMDR works particularly well with phobias that have a clear origin—a specific event that sparked the fear.

Flying Phobia

Jennifer was terrified of flying. This was a problem because her job required occasional travel, and her family lived across the country. She'd been avoiding flights for three years, making excuses, driving long distances instead, or simply missing events she couldn't drive to.

In EMDR, Jennifer traced her fear back to a flight when she was 22. The plane hit severe turbulence. Oxygen masks dropped. The pilot had to make an emergency landing. Everyone was fine, but Jennifer was traumatized. After that flight, she couldn't get on a plane without panicking.

Using EMDR, Jennifer processed the memory of that turbulent flight. During processing, she recognized that the plane had actually been fine—it had handled the situation exactly as designed. She connected with the fact that she'd flown dozens of times before and after that incident without problems. She realized the pilots were trained for these situations.

After three EMDR sessions, Jennifer was able to book a flight. She was nervous (that's normal), but she wasn't panicking. She got on the plane. She didn't enjoy the flight, but she made it through without overwhelming anxiety. With each subsequent flight, it got easier.

Needle Phobia

Brandon's fear of needles was so severe he'd avoided doctors for years. He hadn't had bloodwork done in over a decade. He needed vaccinations but couldn't bring himself to get them. Even thinking about needles made him feel faint.

EMDR helped Brandon process a traumatic medical experience from childhood. When he was seven, he'd been hospitalized for several days. The nurses had a hard time finding his veins and had to stick him repeatedly. He remembered crying and feeling helpless while adults held him down.

That experience had created a deep fear response that continued into adulthood. After processing this memory with EMDR, Brandon's needle phobia significantly decreased. He was able to get necessary bloodwork and vaccinations. He still didn't enjoy needles (who does?), but he wasn't terrified of them anymore.

Dog Phobia

Remember Diana from the earlier chapter? She'd been bitten by a dog at age eight and was still terrified of dogs at age 28. EMDR helped her reprocess that attack. She came to recognize that one aggressive dog didn't mean all dogs were dangerous. She remembered other experiences with friendly dogs before the attack. She connected with the fact that she was no longer a small, helpless child—she was an adult who could protect herself if needed.

After EMDR, Diana still had a healthy respect for unknown dogs, but she could be around friends' dogs without panic. She could walk past dogs on the street without crossing to the other side. The phobia no longer controlled her life.

Grief and Loss: When Mourning Gets Stuck

Grief is a natural response to loss. It's not a disorder or a problem. But sometimes grief gets complicated by trauma surrounding the loss, or old losses trigger grief that never got fully processed.

When Oscar's wife died after a long battle with cancer, he expected to grieve. What he didn't expect was that his grief would become so overwhelming he couldn't function. Two years after her death, he still couldn't go through her belongings. He couldn't visit her grave. Thinking about her sent him into such despair he had to distract himself immediately.

Oscar's therapist helped him recognize that his grief was complicated by traumatic memories of her suffering during the illness. Every time he tried to remember his wife, his brain went to images of her in pain, weak, dying. Those traumatic memories blocked access to the good memories of their 30 years together.

EMDR helped Oscar process the traumatic memories of her illness and death. This didn't make him stop missing her—grief doesn't work that way. But it allowed him to remember her without being overwhelmed by those final difficult months. He could access happy memories again. He could look at photos without falling apart. He could visit her grave.

Oscar still missed his wife. He still felt sad. But the grief became manageable instead of overwhelming.

Performance Anxiety: Fear of Failure

Performance anxiety shows up in many forms—test anxiety, fear of public speaking, stage fright, athletic performance anxiety, sexual performance anxiety.

Gina was a talented violinist. She played beautifully when practicing alone or with her teacher. But in recitals or auditions, she fell apart. Her hands shook. Her mind went blank. She'd make mistakes she never made in practice.

This anxiety was holding her back from a professional music career she'd trained years for.

Through EMDR, Gina traced this back to a piano recital when she was nine. She'd forgotten part of her piece, stopped playing, and run off stage crying while the audience stared. The humiliation of that moment had been seared into her brain.

Even though Gina was now 24, an accomplished musician who'd played successfully many times since then, her brain still treated performance situations as threatening. That childhood memory was still active, still triggering the anxiety response.

After processing that memory with EMDR, Gina's performance anxiety dramatically decreased. She could feel nervous excitement before performances (which actually enhances performance) without the overwhelming anxiety that had been sabotaging her.

Low Self-Esteem and Negative Self-Beliefs

Sometimes people struggle with pervasive negative beliefs about themselves—"I'm not good enough," "I'm worthless," "I'm unlovable," "I'm stupid," "I'm powerless." These beliefs often come from early experiences of criticism, rejection, abuse, or failure.

Tyler had always felt like he wasn't good enough. He worked incredibly hard, achieved a lot, but never felt satisfied. No matter what he accomplished, that voice in his head said, "Not good enough."

29

In EMDR, Tyler identified several memories that seemed to feed this belief:

- His father constantly criticizing him as a child
- Being the last one picked for teams in gym class
- His older brother being the "successful" one the family praised
- A harsh teacher in third grade who told him he'd never amount to anything

These experiences, especially repeated over time, had created a core belief that Tyler was inadequate. Even though adult Tyler was objectively successful—good job, healthy relationships, multiple accomplishments—that childhood-formed belief continued to drive him.

EMDR helped Tyler reprocess these memories. He recognized his father's criticism reflected his father's own issues, not Tyler's worth. He saw that being picked last in childhood gym class had no bearing on his value as a person. He could appreciate his brother's successes without that diminishing his own. He realized that teacher's comment said more about the teacher than about him.

As these memories were reprocessed, Tyler's self-esteem improved. He could acknowledge his accomplishments without immediately discounting them. The constant feeling of "not good enough" began to fade.

What EMDR Cannot Fix

It's important to be realistic about EMDR's limitations. EMDR is powerful for addressing problems rooted in unprocessed memories, but it's not a cure-all.

EMDR probably won't help if:

The problem is primarily biological or genetic. If someone has depression that runs strongly in their family with no clear traumatic origin, EMDR probably won't resolve it. If someone has bipolar disorder, schizophrenia, or other conditions with a strong biological basis, EMDR won't treat the underlying condition (though it might help with any trauma the person has experienced).

The problem is ongoing, not in the past. EMDR works on past memories. If you're currently in an abusive relationship, EMDR can't fix that—you need to get to safety first. If you're dealing with current, ongoing stress (a difficult divorce, caring for a sick family member, job stress), EMDR isn't designed to handle present-day situations. It might be helpful later, after the situation is resolved, but it's not a tool for current crises.

There's no memory component. Some problems genuinely don't have roots in past experiences. Sometimes anxiety is just chemical. Sometimes depression doesn't link to specific events. EMDR won't help in these cases because there are no memories to reprocess.

The person isn't ready. EMDR requires a certain level of stability and ability to handle difficult emotions. Someone in acute crisis, someone actively suicidal, someone with severe dissociation that isn't managed—these situations need to be stabilized first before EMDR can be safely used.

How Do You Know If EMDR Might Help You?

Ask yourself these questions:

1. Is your current problem connected to past experiences? (Even if you're not sure exactly which experiences, do you sense a connection to your past?)
2. Do certain situations trigger you in ways that seem out of proportion to what's actually happening?
3. Do you have intrusive memories, nightmares, or flashbacks?
4. Have you tried other treatments that helped somewhat but didn't fully resolve the issue?
5. Do you avoid certain situations, places, or activities because they trigger anxiety or other difficult emotions?

6. Do you have negative beliefs about yourself ("I'm not good enough," "I'm not safe," "I can't trust anyone") that seem tied to past experiences?

If you answered yes to several of these, EMDR might be worth exploring.

EMDR's Growing Applications

Researchers and therapists continue finding new applications for EMDR. It's being used for:

- Chronic pain with a traumatic origin
- Eating disorders rooted in trauma
- Addiction when past trauma drives the substance use
- Dissociative disorders
- Complicated grief
- Body dysmorphic disorder
- Some personality disorders

The common thread: When current symptoms are driven by unprocessed past experiences, EMDR can help.

EMDR is best known for treating PTSD, but it helps with much more. Anxiety, depression, phobias, grief, performance issues, low self-esteem—all of these can be addressed with EMDR when they're rooted in unprocessed memories.

The key question is: Are your current problems driven by past experiences that your brain hasn't fully processed? If so, EMDR might be the missing piece you've been looking for.

In the next chapter, we'll walk through exactly what happens during EMDR treatment—the eight phases that take you from identifying the problem to full resolution.

CHAPTER 4: The 8 Phases of EMDR Therapy

EMDR isn't just "think about trauma while moving your eyes." It's a comprehensive, eight-phase treatment protocol that was carefully developed and has been refined over three decades. Each phase serves a specific purpose, and skipping phases or rushing through them can reduce EMDR's effectiveness or even cause harm.

Think of EMDR like building a house. You can't just start putting up walls. You need a foundation first, then framing, then walls, then a roof. Each step builds on the previous one. The eight phases of EMDR work the same way.

Let's walk through each phase so you know exactly what to expect.

Phase 1: History Taking and Treatment Planning

This is where it all starts. Your first EMDR session (or first few sessions) won't involve any trauma processing. Instead, your therapist needs to get to know you and your history.

What happens in this phase:

Your therapist will ask about your current symptoms and problems. What brought you to therapy? What are you struggling with? They'll also ask about your history—your childhood, significant life events, traumas you've experienced, your relationships, your strengths and resources.

This isn't just small talk. Your therapist is building a map of how your brain's memory networks are organized. They're identifying which memories might be driving your current symptoms. They're also assessing whether you're ready for EMDR or if you need some preparatory work first.

Jordan's experience:

When Jordan first met with an EMDR therapist, he wanted to jump right into processing his military trauma. He'd read about EMDR online and was eager to start. But his therapist spent the entire first session just talking with him, asking questions about his history.

Jordan shared that he'd been in combat in Iraq, had witnessed several deaths, and had been injured in an explosion. He talked about his current symptoms—nightmares, hypervigilance, difficulty connecting with his family. He also talked about his childhood (mostly positive), his marriage (strained but strong), and his support system (a few close friends who understood).

His therapist asked about his coping skills. How did Jordan handle stress? What helped him calm down when upset? Did he have any history of addiction or self-harm?

By the end of the session, Jordan's therapist had a clear picture of his trauma history and current symptoms. She also had a treatment plan: They'd start by strengthening Jordan's coping skills (Phase 2), then target three specific combat memories that seemed to be driving most of his symptoms.

Why this phase matters:

You can't treat what you don't understand. This phase ensures your therapist knows what they're working with and has a clear plan. It also helps identify if there are any safety concerns that need to be addressed before diving into trauma processing.

Some people have such severe symptoms or such limited coping skills that they need to stabilize first. Some people have ongoing threats in their life (like current domestic violence) that need to be addressed before working on past trauma. This phase identifies those issues.

Phase 2: Preparation

This phase is all about getting you ready for the actual trauma processing. For some people, this phase is quick—maybe one session. For others, especially those with complex trauma or limited coping skills, it might take several sessions.

What happens in this phase:

Your therapist will explain how EMDR works, what to expect, and answer all your questions. They'll also teach you specific techniques to help you manage emotions that might come up during or between sessions.

Common preparation techniques include:

The Safe Place/Calm Place Exercise: Your therapist guides you to imagine a place (real or imagined) where you feel completely safe and calm. This could be a beach, a forest, a cozy room—anywhere that feels peaceful to you. You practice bringing up this image while doing bilateral stimulation. This creates a resource you can use if you become too distressed during processing.

The Container Technique: You learn to imagine a container (a box, a safe, a vault) where you can temporarily "store" difficult feelings when you need to function in daily life. This isn't about suppressing emotions, but about having control over when you deal with them.

The Light Stream or Safe Place Exercise: Techniques for self-soothing and emotional regulation that you can use between sessions.

Your therapist will also teach you about the Subjective Units of Disturbance Scale (SUDS), which you'll use throughout treatment. It's a simple 0-10 scale where 0 means no disturbance and 10 means the worst disturbance you can imagine.

Amara's experience:

Amara came to EMDR after years of childhood abuse. She had a hard time managing her emotions. When something upset her, she'd either shut down completely or explode in anger. There wasn't much in between.

Her therapist knew that Amara needed to build better emotion regulation skills before they could safely process trauma. They spent four sessions in the preparation phase.

Amara learned the Safe Place exercise. She imagined her grandmother's garden, a place where she'd felt loved and protected as a child. She practiced bringing up this image with bilateral stimulation until she could access those calm feelings on command.

She learned the Container technique. When difficult memories or feelings came up at work or during family time, she practiced imagining putting them in a sturdy container that she could come back to during therapy.

Her therapist also taught her grounding techniques—ways to stay present in her body and connected to the current moment if she started to dissociate.

These skills weren't just useful for EMDR. Amara used them in her daily life. By the time they finished the preparation phase, she felt more in control of her emotions than she had in years.

Why this phase matters:

Processing trauma can bring up intense emotions. If you don't have skills to manage those emotions, the process can be overwhelming or even harmful. This phase ensures you have the tools you need to handle what comes up.

It's like learning to swim before going into deep water. You need basic skills first.

Phase 3: Assessment

Now we get to the actual trauma processing, starting with assessment. This is where you and your therapist identify specific memories to target and fully set them up for processing.

What happens in this phase:

For each target memory, your therapist will ask you to identify six things:

1. The target memory/image: What's the worst part of the memory? What image represents the entire incident?

For Carlos, who'd been mugged at gunpoint, the target image was the moment the gun was pointed at his face. That single image captured the terror of the entire experience.

2. Negative cognition: What negative belief about yourself goes with that image? These are statements like "I'm powerless," "I'm in danger," "I'm not good enough," "I'm going to die," "I can't trust anyone."

Carlos's negative cognition was "I'm powerless."

3. Positive cognition: What would you rather believe about yourself? What's the positive opposite of that negative belief?

Carlos's positive cognition was "I can handle things" or "I'm capable."

4. Validity of Cognition (VOC): How true does that positive belief feel right now, on a scale of 1-7? (1 = completely false, 7 = completely true)

When Carlos thought about saying "I'm capable" while also thinking about the mugging, it felt completely false. VOC = 1.

5. Emotions: What emotions do you feel when you bring up the memory and the negative belief?

Carlos felt fear and shame.

6. SUDS: How disturbing is this memory right now, on a scale of 0-10?

Carlos rated it as a 9—extremely disturbing.

7. Body sensations: Where do you feel this in your body?

Carlos felt tightness in his chest and a knot in his stomach.

Why all this detail?

This detailed assessment serves several purposes. First, it helps your therapist understand exactly what they're working with. Second, it gives you both a baseline to measure progress against. Third, it helps activate the memory network so that when processing begins, your brain is accessing the right information.

Kayla's experience:

When Kayla started working on her memory of being sexually assaulted in college, she thought the whole memory was equally horrible. But when her therapist asked for the worst part—the image that represented the whole thing—Kayla identified a specific moment: looking up and seeing the door closed, realizing no one was going to help her.

Her negative cognition was "I'm not safe." Her positive cognition was "I'm safe now" or "I can protect myself."

When she tried to feel how true "I'm safe now" felt, it registered as a 2 out of 7—logically she knew she was safe now, but it didn't feel true.

The emotions were terror and shame. Her SUDS rating was 10—the maximum. And physically, she felt it as a crushing weight on her chest and nausea in her stomach.

This assessment gave Kayla's therapist a clear map of what they were working with. It also helped Kayla articulate things she'd never quite put into words before.

Phase 4: Desensitization

This is the heart of EMDR—the actual reprocessing. This is where the bilateral stimulation comes in and where the trauma memory gets processed.

What happens in this phase:

Your therapist will ask you to bring up the target memory—the image, the negative belief, the emotions, and the body sensations. You hold all of that in your awareness. Then your therapist begins the bilateral stimulation.

Usually, this means you follow your therapist's fingers moving back and forth across your field of vision. Your therapist will move their hand back and forth while you follow with your eyes. This typically lasts 20-30 seconds—we call this a "set" of bilateral stimulation.

After each set, your therapist stops and asks, "What do you notice?" or "What's coming up for you?"

You briefly share whatever's arising—a thought, a feeling, a body sensation, a different memory, an image. It doesn't matter what it is. There are no right or wrong answers. You just report what you're experiencing.

Then you do another set of eye movements, focusing on whatever just came up. Your therapist asks again what you notice. You share. Another set of eye movements. And so on.

This continues until the memory is fully processed.

What does "fully processed" mean?

You'll know processing is complete when:

- The SUDS rating drops to 0 or 1 (no disturbance or minimal disturbance)
- The memory feels like "just a memory" rather than something that's still threatening
- You feel emotionally neutral or even positive when you think about it
- New, more adaptive perspectives have emerged

Isaiah's experience:

Isaiah was processing a memory of a car accident where he'd been T-boned at an intersection. He'd been badly injured and his car was totaled. Years later, he still had intense anxiety about driving, especially through intersections.

In the assessment phase, his target image was the moment of impact—seeing the other car about to hit him. His negative cognition was "I'm going to die." His SUDS was a 9.

His therapist asked him to bring up that image while following her fingers. First set of eye movements.

"What do you notice?" his therapist asked.

"I feel the impact again. My chest hurts," Isaiah said.

"Go with that." Another set of eye movements.

"What's coming up now?"

"I'm remembering being trapped in the car. I couldn't get out. I was scared."

"Notice that." Another set.

This continued. Isaiah's brain was processing the memory, moving through it. After several sets, something shifted.

"What do you notice?"

"I just remembered—someone stopped to help me. A woman called 911. She stayed with me until the ambulance came." Isaiah had forgotten this detail.

More sets of eye movements.

"I'm realizing... I survived. I got through it. My body healed."

More processing. Isaiah's SUDS rating gradually dropped. After about 45 minutes of processing, when he brought up the image of the accident, his SUDS was down to a 2. The terror was gone. It felt like something that happened, not something that was still threatening.

They'd finish processing this memory in the next session, but the hardest part was done.

What's happening in your brain during this?

Remember from Chapter 2: The bilateral stimulation seems to activate your brain's natural processing system. As you move through sets of eye movements, your brain is making new connections, integrating new information, and reprocessing the memory.

You might:

- Remember details you'd forgotten
- Gain new perspectives on what happened
- Connect the trauma to other, more positive memories
- Realize things about the situation you hadn't realized before
- Feel the emotional intensity decrease
- Notice body sensations shifting or releasing

41

All of this happens naturally. You're not trying to make it happen. Your therapist isn't telling you what to think. Your brain is doing what it naturally does when given the chance—processing and healing.

How long does this phase take?

It varies widely. A single traumatic event might be fully processed in one 90-minute session. Complex trauma with multiple memories to process might take many sessions over several months.

The processing doesn't have to happen all in one session. If time runs out or you're getting too tired, your therapist will help you close down the session (we'll talk about closure in Phase 7), and you'll continue processing that memory in the next session.

Phase 5: Installation

Once the memory is desensitized (SUDS down to 0 or 1), it's time to install the positive cognition—that positive belief you identified in the assessment phase.

What happens in this phase:

Your therapist asks you to bring up the original memory along with the positive cognition. "When you think about that event, how true does [positive belief] feel now?"

Remember the VOC scale from assessment? You rate how true the positive belief feels, from 1 (completely false) to 7 (completely true).

If it's not a 7, you do sets of bilateral stimulation while holding the memory and the positive belief together, strengthening that connection. The goal is to get the VOC to a 7—where the positive belief feels completely true.

Carlos's installation:

Remember Carlos from the mugging? After desensitization, thinking about the mugging no longer felt terrifying. His SUDS was down to 0. Now it was time to install the positive cognition.

His original positive cognition was "I can handle things." When his therapist asked how true that felt now, with the memory of the mugging, Carlos said it felt pretty true—about a 6.

They did several sets of eye movements while Carlos held the memory along with the belief "I can handle things." With each set, it felt more true. After a few sets, it was a solid 7. When Carlos brought up the memory of the mugging and said "I can handle things," it felt completely true.

What changed? Through the desensitization phase, Carlos's brain had reprocessed the memory and made new connections. He'd reconnected with the fact that he'd survived, that he'd cooperated intelligently to stay alive, that he'd handled the aftermath, that he'd moved forward with his life. The memory no longer meant "I'm powerless." Now it was integrated into his life story as evidence that he actually can handle difficult things.

Why installation matters:

It's not enough to just remove the negative charge from a memory. EMDR also strengthens positive, adaptive beliefs. This creates lasting change. You're not just getting rid of something bad; you're building something good.

Phase 6: Body Scan

Trauma lives in the body as well as the mind. Even after the memory is desensitized and the positive belief is installed, sometimes residual tension or discomfort remains in the body. This phase clears that out.

What happens in this phase:

Your therapist asks you to bring up the original memory along with the positive cognition, and then scan through your body from head to toe. "Do you notice any tension, discomfort, or unusual sensations anywhere?"

If everything feels clear and comfortable, great. Processing is complete. If you notice any tension or discomfort, you target that with more bilateral stimulation until it clears.

Why this matters:

The body keeps score. Sometimes cognitive processing happens, the emotions clear, but the body is still holding tension from the trauma. This phase ensures complete processing.

Naomi's body scan:

Naomi had processed a memory of being in an abusive relationship. The memory was desensitized, the positive belief was installed, everything seemed good. But during the body scan, she noticed tightness in her throat.

They did several sets of eye movements while Naomi focused on that throat tightness. An image came up—her ex-boyfriend yelling at her, telling her to shut up. Her brain was still holding that command in her throat.

More processing. The throat tension gradually released. By the end, Naomi's body felt completely clear.

Phase 7: Closure

Every EMDR session needs to end safely, whether or not processing is complete. This phase ensures you can leave the session stable and able to function in your daily life.

What happens in this phase:

If processing is complete (memory fully desensitized, positive cognition installed, body scan clear), your therapist will acknowledge the good work you did and remind you how to use the self-soothing techniques from Phase 2 if needed during the week.

If processing isn't complete—maybe time ran out, or the memory is partially processed but not finished—your therapist will guide you through techniques to contain the memory until the next session. Remember the Container technique from Phase 2? This is where it comes in handy.

Your therapist will also brief you on what might happen between sessions. Sometimes processing continues between sessions. You might have dreams, new memories might surface, or you might notice emotions bubbling up. This is normal. It's your brain continuing the healing process.

Vincent's closure:

Vincent was processing a memory of witnessing a violent crime. By the end of the session, his SUDS was down from a 9 to a 4— significant progress, but not complete. They'd run out of time for that session.

His therapist helped him use the Container technique to temporarily set aside the memory. Vincent imagined putting the memory in a sturdy safe with a combination lock. He could come back to it in their next session, but for now, it was secured.

His therapist reminded him to use his Safe Place exercise if he needed it during the week. She also told him to keep a log of any dreams, memories, or thoughts that came up related to the trauma they were working on.

The next week, Vincent came back and reported that he'd had a couple of dreams about the incident, but they weren't nightmares— more like his brain working through it. They resumed processing, and within another 30 minutes, the memory was fully resolved.

Phase 8: Re-evaluation

This happens at the beginning of each new session after you've done processing work. Your therapist checks to make sure the previous session's work has held and that you're ready to continue.

What happens in this phase:

Your therapist asks you to bring up the memory you processed last time. "When you think about that now, what's your SUDS?" If it's still at 0 or 1, great—that memory is done. If the SUDS has gone back up, you need to do more processing on that memory.

Your therapist also checks if any new material has emerged—new memories, new aspects of the old memory, related issues that came up during the week.

The complete cycle:

Let me walk you through what a complete EMDR treatment might look like, using Emma's treatment for social anxiety.

Session 1-2: History and Preparation (Phases 1-2) Emma told her therapist about her severe social anxiety. Through history taking, they identified several memories that seemed connected: being mocked in middle school, a humiliating experience at a party in college, and critical parents who often embarrassed her in front of others.

They spent a session on preparation. Emma learned the Safe Place exercise (she imagined a quiet library) and the Container technique. She learned about SUDS and VOC scales.

Session 3: Assessment and First Processing (Phases 3-4) They started with the middle school memory—being laughed at during a presentation. Assessment: Image = classmates laughing, pointing. Negative cognition = "I'm ridiculous." Positive cognition = "I'm

46

acceptable as I am." VOC = 2. Emotions = shame, fear. SUDS = 8. Body sensation = burning in her face.

They began processing. After 45 minutes, Emma's SUDS was down to a 3. Time was up, so they did closure, using the Container technique.

Session 4: Continued Processing and Installation (Phases 4-5)
Re-evaluation: The memory was still a 3. They resumed processing. Within 20 minutes, it was down to 0. Installation: "I'm acceptable as I am" went from a 6 to a 7. Body scan: all clear. Closure: Emma felt good. The memory was fully processed.

Sessions 5-8: Processing Additional Memories They worked through the college party incident and several memories of parental criticism. Each memory went through the same phases: assessment, desensitization, installation, body scan, closure, re-evaluation.

Session 9: Integration and Future Template All target memories were processed. Emma's social anxiety had dramatically decreased. They spent this session creating a "future template"—practicing how Emma would handle upcoming social situations with her new, healthier responses.

Follow-up sessions: Emma continued therapy for a few more sessions to work on building social skills and addressing any remaining issues, but the trauma processing was complete.

What Makes EMDR Different from Other Therapies

These eight phases might sound like a lot of structure, but that's actually one of EMDR's strengths. You're not just venting about trauma endlessly. You're moving through a specific, proven protocol designed to produce resolution.

Unlike traditional talk therapy where you might discuss the same issues for years, EMDR moves through material efficiently. Unlike exposure therapy where you repeatedly re-experience the trauma in detail, EMDR requires only brief activation of the memory. The bilateral stimulation does the work.

Key Takeaways

The eight phases of EMDR provide a roadmap from identifying the problem to complete resolution:

1. History Taking - Understanding your story
2. Preparation - Building your skills and resources
3. Assessment - Setting up the target memory
4. Desensitization - Processing the memory with bilateral stimulation
5. Installation - Strengthening the positive belief
6. Body Scan - Clearing any residual tension
7. Closure - Ending safely
8. Re-evaluation - Checking that the work held

Each phase builds on the previous ones. The structure ensures safety and effectiveness. And while it might sound complicated when written out like this, when you're actually going through it with a trained therapist, the process flows naturally.

In the next chapter, we'll talk about what your first EMDR session will actually be like and how to prepare for it, including how to find a qualified therapist and what questions to ask.

CHAPTER 5: What to Expect: Your First EMDR Session and Beyond

So you've decided to try EMDR. Maybe you're excited. Maybe you're nervous. Maybe you're skeptical but willing to give it a shot. Whatever you're feeling, it helps to know exactly what you're getting into.

Let's walk through the entire process, from finding a therapist to what happens after your treatment is complete.

Finding a Qualified EMDR Therapist

Not every therapist who knows about EMDR is qualified to provide it. EMDR requires specific training beyond a standard therapy degree. Here's what you need to know about finding someone qualified.

Training Levels:

EMDR therapists can have different levels of training:

EMDR-Trained: This therapist has completed the basic EMDR training, which is typically 40-50 hours of instruction plus supervised practice. This is the minimum qualification you want. Many excellent EMDR therapists have this level of training and nothing more—and that's perfectly fine.

EMDR-Certified: This therapist has completed additional requirements beyond basic training, including 50 hours of continuing education in EMDR, 2 years of experience using EMDR, consultation hours, and a written exam. Certification shows dedication, but remember—many great EMDR therapists aren't certified. It's a plus, not a requirement.

EMDR Consultant: This therapist is qualified to train and supervise other EMDR therapists. This is the highest level, but again, you don't necessarily need someone at this level. A well-trained, experienced EMDR therapist without consultant status can do excellent work.

Where to Look:

The EMDR International Association (EMDRIA) has a therapist directory on their website: www.emdria.org. You can search by location and see each therapist's training level, specialties, and contact information.

You can also search general therapist directories like Psychology Today, filtering for EMDR as a specialty.

Ask your regular doctor or your current therapist (if you have one) for referrals. Word of mouth from people you trust can be valuable.

What to Look For:

Beyond EMDR training, consider these factors:

Experience with your specific issue: If you're dealing with combat trauma, look for someone experienced with veterans. If you're working on childhood abuse, find someone who specializes in complex trauma. If you have a phobia, look for someone who's successfully treated phobias.

License and credentials: Your therapist should be a licensed mental health professional—a psychologist, clinical social worker, licensed professional counselor, or psychiatrist. EMDR training doesn't replace the need for basic mental health credentials.

Practical considerations: Location, cost, insurance acceptance, availability. The best therapist in the world won't help if you can't afford them or can't get to their office.

Personal fit: You need to feel comfortable with this person. EMDR requires trust. If something feels off during your consultation, it's okay to keep looking.

Lily's search:

Lily wanted EMDR for her driving phobia after a serious accident. She searched the EMDRIA directory for therapists in her area. She found five names and looked up each one online.

Two didn't take her insurance, so she eliminated them. One had very limited availability that didn't match her schedule. That left two candidates.

She called both for brief phone consultations. The first therapist was pleasant but hadn't worked much with phobias—her main experience was with combat trauma. The second therapist had successfully treated several clients with driving phobias using EMDR. Lily scheduled an intake appointment with her.

At that first meeting, Lily asked:

- "How much of your practice involves EMDR?"
- "How many clients with driving phobias have you treated?"
- "What's your success rate with phobias?"
- "How long do you typically work with phobia clients?"

The therapist answered all her questions straightforwardly. Lily felt comfortable with her. She decided to move forward.

Questions to Ask During Your Consultation

Before committing to EMDR with a therapist, ask these questions:

About their training and experience:

- "What EMDR training have you completed?"
- "How long have you been practicing EMDR?"

- "Have you worked with clients with [your specific issue]?"
- "What percentage of your practice uses EMDR?"

About the treatment process:

- "How do you structure EMDR sessions?"
- "How many sessions do you typically see for [your issue]?"
- "What happens if I get too overwhelmed during processing?"
- "Do you offer EMDR through telehealth, or only in person?"

About practical matters:

- "What's your fee?"
- "Do you take my insurance?"
- "How long are sessions?"
- "What's your cancellation policy?"
- "How quickly can you usually schedule appointments?"

Red flags to watch for:

- The therapist guarantees results or promises to "cure" you in a specific number of sessions
- They claim EMDR can treat everything
- They seem dismissive of your concerns or questions
- They have no specific training in EMDR but claim they "do something similar"
- They pressure you to commit before you're ready
- Their answers to your questions are vague or evasive

Trust your gut. If something feels wrong, keep looking.

Your First Session: What Actually Happens

Your first EMDR session will likely be all or mostly history-taking (Phase 1). No trauma processing yet. Here's what to expect.

Check-in and paperwork:

You'll probably arrive 10-15 minutes early to complete intake paperwork—basic information, medical history, current medications, emergency contacts, consent forms.

Building rapport:

The first part of the session is about getting to know each other. Your therapist will ask about what brings you in, but they'll also ask about you as a person. This isn't wasted time. EMDR requires trust, and trust requires connection.

Your story:

Your therapist will ask you to describe your current problems. What are you struggling with? When did it start? How does it affect your daily life?

They'll also ask about your history. You don't have to go into graphic detail about traumas, but they need to understand what you've been through. They might ask:

- About your childhood and family
- About significant relationships
- About traumatic events you've experienced
- About previous therapy or treatment
- About your current support system
- About your coping skills and strengths

Assessment of readiness:

Your therapist is also assessing whether you're ready for EMDR. Do you have adequate coping skills? Are you stable enough to handle the emotions that might come up? Are there safety concerns that need to be addressed first?

If you're actively suicidal, in the middle of a crisis, or lacking basic emotional regulation skills, your therapist might recommend doing some preparatory work before starting EMDR processing.

Creating a treatment plan:

By the end of the first session (or first few sessions), your therapist should have a treatment plan. They should be able to tell you:

- What memories or issues you'll target
- What order you'll address them in
- Roughly how long treatment might take
- What to expect from the process

Antonio's first session:

Antonio went to his first EMDR appointment feeling nervous. He'd never been to therapy before. His wife had convinced him to go after his anxiety about his heart attack got so bad he was having panic attacks.

His therapist, Dr. Martinez, greeted him warmly. They sat in comfortable chairs (not the stereotypical therapy couch). Dr. Martinez asked Antonio to tell her what brought him in.

Antonio explained: He'd had a heart attack six months ago. He recovered well physically, but mentally, he was a mess. He was terrified it would happen again. He monitored his heart rate constantly. Every little twinge of chest discomfort sent him into a panic. He'd been to the ER four times thinking he was having another heart attack—it was always just anxiety.

Dr. Martinez asked questions. What was the heart attack like? What was most frightening about it? How had it changed his life? She also asked about Antonio's childhood (generally happy), his marriage (strong), his job (stressful but manageable), and his coping skills (he used to exercise to manage stress but was now too scared to exercise).

She explained that EMDR could help him process the trauma of the heart attack so it stopped controlling his present life. She outlined what treatment would look like: A session or two of preparation, then processing the memory of the heart attack, then possibly some work on his health anxiety more broadly.

Antonio left that first session feeling hopeful. He had a plan. He understood what would happen next. And he liked Dr. Martinez—she'd listened without judgment and seemed to genuinely understand what he was going through.

The Preparation Session: Building Your Toolkit

Depending on your situation, you might have one preparation session or several. This is where you learn the skills you'll need to handle EMDR processing safely.

What you'll learn:

The Safe Place/Calm Place exercise: Your therapist will guide you through creating a mental image of a place where you feel completely safe and calm. This can be a real place you've been or an imaginary place.

Let's say you choose a beach you visited as a kid. Your therapist will ask you to imagine it in detail—the sound of the waves, the feel of the sand, the smell of salt air, the warmth of the sun. You practice bringing up this image until you can feel the calm it produces.

Then your therapist adds bilateral stimulation. You imagine the beach while following their finger or using the tappers. This strengthens the association between the bilateral stimulation and the feeling of calm. Now you have a resource you can use if processing gets too intense.

The Container technique: You learn to imagine a secure container—a safe, a vault, a locked box, whatever feels secure to you. This is where you can temporarily "put" difficult feelings or memories when you need to function in daily life.

This isn't about avoiding your feelings. It's about having control over when you deal with them. If a difficult memory comes up on Tuesday morning before work, you can "contain" it until your Thursday therapy session.

Grounding techniques: Your therapist teaches you ways to stay present if you start to dissociate or feel overwhelmed. This might include:

- The 5-4-3-2-1 technique: Name 5 things you can see, 4 things you can touch, 3 things you can hear, 2 things you can smell, 1 thing you can taste
- Holding ice cubes or splashing cold water on your face
- Stomping your feet on the ground to feel the connection to the floor
- Orienting yourself to the present: saying out loud where you are, what year it is, how old you are now

Understanding SUDS and VOC: Your therapist explains the rating scales you'll use throughout treatment. The SUDS scale (0-10 for disturbance) and the VOC scale (1-7 for how true a positive belief feels).

Realistic expectations: Your therapist should also prepare you for what processing might feel like. It might be uncomfortable. You might cry or feel angry or scared. But you'll never be out of control. You can always stop if you need to. And those difficult feelings are temporary—they're part of the healing process, not something to be afraid of.

Bethany's preparation:

Bethany was starting EMDR for childhood trauma. She'd been abused by a family member from ages 6 to 10. She'd been in therapy off and on for years but had never fully processed what happened.

Her EMDR therapist, Janice, spent two full sessions on preparation before doing any trauma processing.

In the first preparation session, Bethany learned the Safe Place exercise. Her safe place was an imaginary treehouse—a place she'd dreamed about as a child but never had. In her mind, this treehouse was in a huge oak tree, high above the ground where no one could reach her. It had soft cushions, warm sunlight filtering through the leaves, and a lock on the door that only she controlled.

Bethany practiced bringing up this image. At first, it was hard—her mind would wander or intrusive memories would interrupt. But with practice and bilateral stimulation, she got better at accessing the calm feeling of her safe treehouse.

In the second preparation session, Bethany learned the Container technique. She imagined a bank vault with a huge metal door and a complex combination only she knew. She practiced "putting" difficult memories in the vault and closing the door.

Janice also taught Bethany grounding techniques because Bethany had a tendency to dissociate when things got overwhelming. They practiced the 5-4-3-2-1 technique and the ice cube technique.

By the end of those two sessions, Bethany had a toolkit. She felt more prepared to handle whatever came up during processing.

Your First Processing Session: The Real Deal

Now we get to actual trauma processing. Here's what that first processing session typically looks like.

Setup:

You'll sit in a comfortable chair. Your therapist will sit across from you or slightly to the side. If you're using eye movements, you need to be positioned so you can easily follow your therapist's hand. If you're using tappers or headphones, they'll get those set up.

Target selection:

Your therapist will remind you which memory you're starting with (this was decided during treatment planning). They'll walk you through the assessment phase: identifying the image, the negative cognition, the positive cognition, rating the VOC, identifying the emotions, rating the SUDS, and noting body sensations.

First set of bilateral stimulation:

Your therapist will say something like, "Bring up that image, along with the words [negative cognition] and where you feel it in your body. Now follow my fingers."

They'll move their hand back and forth across your field of vision. You follow with your eyes. This typically lasts 20-30 seconds. It might feel weird at first—following someone's hand back and forth while thinking about trauma is an unusual experience.

The check-in:

Your therapist stops the eye movements and asks, "What do you notice?" or "What's coming up?"

You briefly share whatever arose during that set. Maybe the image became more vivid. Maybe a new thought popped up. Maybe you felt a body sensation. Maybe a different memory came to mind. Maybe the emotion intensified or decreased. Whatever happened, you share it briefly—this isn't the time for a long explanation.

More sets:

Your therapist says, "Go with that" or "Notice that," and starts another set of eye movements. After that set, another check-in. Then another set. And so on.

This continues, with your processing moving wherever your brain takes it. Your therapist is following your lead, letting your brain do what it needs to do.

What processing feels like:

This varies dramatically from person to person and even from session to session. Some people describe it as:

- Like watching a movie of the memory that gradually speeds up and becomes less intense
- Like the memory is moving further away, becoming smaller
- Like releasing something heavy they've been carrying
- Like pieces of a puzzle clicking into place
- Like waking up from a bad dream

Processing can be emotional. You might cry. You might feel angry. You might feel scared. That's okay. Your therapist is there to help you through it. And remember, you're not reliving the trauma— you're processing it. There's a difference.

Duration:

The actual processing portion of a session might last 30-60 minutes. Some memories process quickly—you might completely resolve a single incident trauma in one session. Other memories, especially if they're complex or part of a pattern of trauma, might take several sessions to fully process.

Cameron's first processing session:

Cameron was processing his memory of a car accident where his best friend died. Cameron had been driving. It wasn't his fault— another driver ran a red light—but Cameron blamed himself. For three years, he'd been carrying guilt, playing the accident over and over in his mind, thinking about all the "what ifs."

During assessment, Cameron's target image was the moment right after impact—seeing his friend slumped over, knowing something was terribly wrong. His negative cognition was "I should have saved him." His positive cognition was "I did everything I could." VOC

59

was a 2. His emotions were guilt and grief. SUDS was a 10. Body sensation was a crushing weight on his chest.

The therapist had Cameron bring up the image while doing eye movements. First set.

"What do you notice?"

"I see the impact. I hear the sound of metal crunching. I feel the weight on my chest."

"Go with that." Another set.

"What's coming up?"

"I'm remembering trying to check on him. I couldn't unbuckle his seatbelt. I was trying to help but everything was wrong."

"Notice that." Another set.

This continued. Cameron moved through the memory. He cried. He felt the grief and guilt intensely. But as the sets continued, something started to shift.

"I'm remembering—the paramedics said he died instantly. There was nothing anyone could have done. They told me that at the hospital, but I didn't really hear it then."

More sets.

"I'm thinking about how he wouldn't want me to feel like this. He was always telling me not to be so hard on myself."

More sets.

"The other driver ran the light. I looked. I checked. I did everything right. It wasn't my fault."

Cameron's SUDS rating gradually dropped. By the end of the session, it was down to a 5—still present, but significantly reduced. They'd continue in the next session.

Cameron left that session exhausted but lighter. For the first time in three years, he felt like he might actually be able to move past this.

Between Sessions: What to Expect

EMDR doesn't just happen in the therapy office. Your brain continues processing between sessions. Here's what might happen and how to handle it.

Continued processing:

You might notice:

- Dreams about the trauma or related issues (not necessarily nightmares, just your brain working through material)
- Memories you'd forgotten suddenly coming to mind
- Emotions bubbling up seemingly out of nowhere
- Insights or new perspectives occurring to you
- Changes in how you react to triggers

This is all normal and actually a good sign. It means your brain's processing system is activated and doing its work.

What to do:

Keep a log. Your therapist probably asked you to write down any dreams, memories, or insights that come up. This helps track your progress and gives you material to discuss in your next session.

Use your coping skills. If difficult feelings come up, use the Safe Place exercise or the Container technique. You don't have to process everything immediately. You can contain things until your next session.

Be gentle with yourself. Processing trauma is hard work, even though you're not doing anything that feels like "work." Your brain is reorganizing old information, which takes energy. It's normal to feel tired or emotionally raw for a day or two after processing sessions.

When to call your therapist:

Most between-session experiences are normal and manageable. But call your therapist if:

- You're having suicidal thoughts
- You're feeling overwhelmed and your coping skills aren't helping
- You're afraid you might hurt yourself or someone else
- Something feels very wrong in a way you can't explain

Good EMDR therapists make themselves available for brief check-ins between sessions if needed. You're not bothering them by reaching out.

Dana's between-session experience:

Dana processed a memory of being bullied in high school during her Wednesday session. That night, she had a dream about high school—not a nightmare, just a dream where she was back there. In the dream, she stood up to the bullies in a way she hadn't been able to in real life.

Thursday, she felt a bit emotional but okay. She used her Safe Place exercise once when she started feeling overwhelmed at work.

Friday, a memory popped into her mind that she hadn't thought about in years—a teacher who'd been kind to her during that difficult time. She'd forgotten about Ms. Peterson. Remembering her brought tears to Dana's eyes, but good tears. Ms. Peterson had told Dana she was smart and capable and had a bright future. Dana wrote this memory down to tell her therapist.

By Saturday, Dana felt different. Lighter. Less burdened by that old shame. When she went to a social event Saturday night—something that usually made her anxious—she felt more comfortable than she had in years.

How Long Does EMDR Take?

This is the question everyone wants answered, and unfortunately, the answer is: it depends.

For a single-incident trauma:

If you experienced one specific traumatic event and you're otherwise stable with good coping skills, EMDR might take 3-12 sessions. Often, a single traumatic memory can be fully processed in 1-3 sessions, but you might need a few additional sessions for related material and to ensure the treatment has fully taken hold.

For complex trauma:

If you experienced ongoing trauma (like childhood abuse that lasted years, or combat deployment with multiple traumatic experiences), treatment takes longer. You might need 12-24 sessions or more. You're not processing one memory; you're processing many related memories.

For other conditions:

Phobias often respond quickly—sometimes in just 3-5 sessions. Anxiety and depression linked to trauma might take 8-15 sessions. It varies based on how many memories are feeding the problem.

What affects treatment length?

- The severity and complexity of the trauma
- Your baseline stability and coping skills
- Whether you have other ongoing stressors

- How well you tolerate processing (some people can do intensive processing, others need to go more slowly)
- The quality of the therapeutic relationship

Typical session frequency:

Most people do EMDR weekly. Some people, especially those with complex trauma, start with weekly sessions but spread them out as treatment progresses. Others do intensive EMDR—multiple sessions per week or even multiple sessions in one day—though this is less common.

Progress isn't always linear:

You might have sessions where you make huge progress, followed by sessions where it feels like nothing's happening. This is normal. Your brain is doing complex work. Trust the process.

What Sessions Actually Cost

Let's talk money, because this matters. EMDR isn't cheap, but there are ways to make it more affordable.

Typical costs:

EMDR therapists typically charge $100-$250 per session, depending on their credentials, experience, and location. Sessions are usually 60-90 minutes.

Insurance:

Many insurance plans cover EMDR if it's provided by a licensed mental health professional for a covered diagnosis (like PTSD, anxiety disorders, or depression). You'll want to check:

- Does your plan cover outpatient mental health services?
- Is the therapist in-network with your insurance?
- What's your copay or coinsurance?

- Do you need preauthorization?
- Is there a session limit?

Some therapists are in-network with insurance companies. Others are out-of-network, meaning you pay upfront and then submit for reimbursement (if your plan covers out-of-network providers).

Sliding scale:

Some EMDR therapists offer sliding scale fees based on income. It doesn't hurt to ask, especially if you're paying out of pocket.

Community mental health centers:

Some community mental health centers have staff trained in EMDR and charge on a sliding scale. The wait lists can be long, but the cost is more manageable.

Training clinics:

Universities with psychology or social work programs sometimes have training clinics where graduate students provide EMDR under supervision. The cost is typically lower, though the therapists are less experienced.

Employee assistance programs (EAPs):

If you have an EAP through your employer, you might get several free therapy sessions. Ask if they have EMDR-trained therapists in their network.

In-Person vs. Online EMDR

Traditionally, EMDR was done in person. But especially since 2020, many therapists offer EMDR online through secure video platforms. Does it work as well?

Online EMDR:

Yes, EMDR can be effective online. Your therapist can guide you through bilateral stimulation in several ways:

- Following a moving dot or light on your screen
- Using a smartphone app that provides alternating sounds or vibrations
- Tapping alternately on your own knees or shoulders while the therapist guides you
- Using Bluetooth tappers you purchase

Advantages of online EMDR:

- No travel time
- More therapist options (you're not limited to your geographic area)
- More comfortable for some people to process from home
- Easier to schedule

Disadvantages of online EMDR:

- Technology issues can interrupt processing
- Your therapist can't be physically present if you become very distressed
- Some people find it harder to connect emotionally through a screen
- Privacy concerns if you don't have a private space at home

Which is better?

Neither is inherently better. It's personal preference. Some people love online EMDR. Others strongly prefer in-person. Many therapists offer both options.

Frank's online EMDR experience:

Frank lived in a rural area with no EMDR therapists nearby. The closest was two hours away. He found a therapist three states over who offered online EMDR.

Frank was skeptical at first. How could this work over video? But his therapist walked him through the setup. Frank downloaded an app on his phone that provided alternating tones. During sessions, he'd hold the phone and listen to the alternating sounds while processing.

It worked. Frank successfully processed several combat memories through online EMDR. The distance didn't matter. The technology didn't get in the way. And he could do sessions from his home without the four-hour round-trip drive.

After EMDR: Maintaining Your Progress

Once you've completed EMDR and your target memories are processed, what next?

Recognizing completion:

You'll know treatment is complete when:

- The target memories no longer cause distress
- You can think about what happened without being overwhelmed
- Your symptoms (nightmares, anxiety, avoidance, etc.) have significantly decreased or resolved
- You can handle situations that used to trigger you
- You feel more present in your current life rather than stuck in the past

Follow-up sessions:

Many therapists schedule follow-up sessions 1 month, 3 months, and 6 months after completing the main treatment. This ensures the progress has held and addresses any residual issues.

Maintenance:

The good news is that EMDR's effects tend to last. Once a memory is properly processed, it stays processed. You don't need to keep "working" on it.

However, maintaining general mental health is still important:

- Continue using healthy coping skills
- Maintain your support system
- Take care of your physical health
- Address new stressors promptly rather than letting them build up

New material:

Sometimes after completing EMDR, new memories surface that weren't accessible before. This doesn't mean the treatment failed. Your brain might have been protecting you from memories you weren't ready to handle yet. If new material comes up, you can return to EMDR to process it.

Other therapy:

EMDR processes traumatic memories, but you might benefit from other therapy for other issues. Some people continue with general therapy after EMDR to work on relationship skills, life transitions, or other non-trauma-related concerns.

The Bottom Line

Starting EMDR involves finding a qualified therapist, doing some preparation work, and then processing target memories through a structured protocol. Sessions typically last 60-90 minutes and might continue weekly for several weeks to several months, depending on your needs.

The process might feel strange at first—moving your eyes back and forth while thinking about trauma isn't what most people expect from therapy. But EMDR has helped millions of people find relief from symptoms that other treatments couldn't touch.

In the next chapter, we'll look at real stories from people who've gone through EMDR treatment, so you can see what the full process looks like from start to finish.

CHAPTER 6: Real Stories of Transformation: EMDR Success Cases

Nothing explains EMDR better than hearing from people who've actually been through it. In this chapter, you'll read real accounts of how EMDR changed lives. These stories show different types of trauma, different symptoms, and different paths to healing.

Story 1: Marcus - Combat Veteran with PTSD

The Problem:

Marcus served in the Army for eight years, including two deployments to Afghanistan. He left the military at age 29 and tried to return to civilian life. It didn't go well.

He couldn't sleep more than three hours without waking from nightmares. Loud noises made him hit the ground. He couldn't go to crowded places because he was constantly scanning for threats. He was irritable and angry all the time, snapping at his wife and kids over small things. He started drinking to numb the feelings. He isolated himself, pulling away from friends and family.

His wife finally gave him an ultimatum: get help or she'd take the kids and leave. Marcus went to the VA. He tried regular talk therapy. It helped him understand PTSD, but his symptoms didn't improve much. After six months, his therapist suggested EMDR.

Marcus was skeptical. Moving his eyes back and forth was going to fix combat trauma? It sounded ridiculous. But he was desperate. He agreed to try.

The Treatment:

Marcus's EMDR therapist asked him to list the worst memories from his deployments. There were several:

70

- An IED explosion that killed two guys in his unit
- A firefight where he thought he was going to die
- Seeing a dead child during a patrol
- The guilt of leaving his unit when his enlistment ended

They started with the IED memory because it was the one that haunted him most. During assessment, Marcus's worst image was seeing the vehicle explode. His negative belief: "I should have saved them." His positive belief: "I did everything I could." His SUDS was a 10. His body was tense all over.

The processing was intense. Marcus cried for the first time since the deployment. He felt rage. He felt grief. His therapist kept him grounded, kept him moving through the bilateral stimulation.

After the first session processing this memory, Marcus's SUDS was down to a 6. Still there, but reduced. He continued processing this memory in the next session. New perspectives emerged. He remembered that the explosion was instantaneous—his friends didn't suffer. He realized there was nothing he could have done differently—it was an ambush. He connected with the fact that his friends wouldn't want him to destroy his life with guilt.

By the third session, the IED memory was fully processed. SUDS at 0. When Marcus thought about it, he felt sad but not destroyed. It was a terrible thing that happened, but it didn't control him anymore.

They moved on to the other memories. The firefight, the dead child, the guilt about leaving. One by one, they processed these memories over the next several months.

The Results:

After six months of EMDR (about 20 sessions), Marcus's life looked completely different.

The nightmares stopped. He slept through the night most nights. When he did dream about Afghanistan, the dreams weren't terrifying—they were just dreams.

The hypervigilance decreased dramatically. He could go to the grocery store without panicking. Loud noises startled him but didn't send him diving for cover.

He stopped drinking. He didn't need alcohol to numb his feelings anymore because the feelings weren't overwhelming.

He reconnected with his wife and kids. He could be present with them instead of being mentally stuck in Afghanistan.

"I can still remember everything that happened," Marcus explained. "The memories are all there. But they don't hurt anymore. It's like they used to be in bright, burning colors that seared my brain. Now they're faded photographs. Still there, but not on fire."

Two years after completing EMDR, Marcus is doing well. He works in construction, coaches his son's soccer team, and goes on regular date nights with his wife. He occasionally has a hard day, but the PTSD doesn't control his life.

Story 2: Jennifer - Sexual Assault Survivor

The Problem:

Jennifer was sexually assaulted at a party during her junior year of college. She was 20 years old. The assault happened in a bedroom at a house party. Someone she knew and had trusted attacked her. She reported it to campus police, but the case went nowhere.

The trauma changed everything. Jennifer couldn't focus on her classes. She stopped going to parties. She stopped dating entirely. She had panic attacks when she was alone with men, even men she knew were safe. She started having nightmares. She blamed herself—she'd been drinking, she'd gone to that room voluntarily (before the assault), maybe she'd somehow asked for it.

She finished college, barely, and moved back home. Five years passed. Jennifer was 25 and still struggling. She'd tried therapy a few times but always quit after a few sessions because talking about what happened made her feel worse, not better.

A friend who'd done EMDR suggested Jennifer try it. Jennifer was hesitant—another therapy that probably wouldn't work—but she scheduled an appointment.

The Treatment:

Jennifer's EMDR therapist spent two full sessions just building rapport and doing preparation work. Jennifer learned the Safe Place exercise (she imagined her grandmother's garden) and the Container technique.

When they started processing, Jennifer didn't have to describe the assault in detail. Her therapist just needed to know what the target memory was. The worst image: looking at the closed door and realizing no one was coming to help her. The negative belief: "I'm not safe." The positive belief: "I'm safe now" or "I can protect myself."

Jennifer's SUDS was a 10. The emotions were terror and shame. She felt it as pressure on her chest and nausea.

The first processing session was difficult. Jennifer shook. She cried. But her therapist kept her grounded. "You're safe here. You're in my office. It's 2023. That was 2018. You survived. You're here."

As Jennifer processed, new insights emerged. She realized the assault wasn't her fault—the attacker made a choice to assault her. Her drinking didn't cause it. Going into that room didn't cause it. His choice caused it.

She remembered that she'd fought back more than she'd previously remembered. She'd said no. She'd tried to push him away. She hadn't just frozen—she'd resisted.

She connected with the fact that she was no longer that 20-year-old college junior. She was 25, stronger, wiser, more able to protect herself.

Processing this memory took four sessions. Each session, the intensity decreased. The shame began to lift. The terror began to fade.

After the memory was fully processed, they worked on related issues—her fear of being alone with men, her panic attacks, her negative beliefs about herself.

The Results:

After four months of EMDR (about 15 sessions), Jennifer's symptoms were mostly gone.

She no longer had panic attacks when alone with men. She could differentiate between "this specific person hurt me" and "all men are dangerous."

The nightmares stopped. When she did dream about the assault, she was able to wake up, remind herself it was over, and go back to sleep.

The shame lifted. Jennifer stopped blaming herself. She understood that what happened was something done to her, not something she caused.

She started dating again. It was scary at first, but she could handle the fear. She set boundaries. She trusted her instincts. When a relationship wasn't healthy, she could leave instead of staying out of fear of being alone.

"EMDR gave me my life back," Jennifer said. "For five years, I was stuck in that room at that party. EMDR helped me get out. The assault is part of my history now, but it's not who I am."

Story 3: Tyler - Childhood Abuse and Low Self-Esteem

The Problem:

Tyler grew up with a father who was extremely critical. Nothing Tyler did was ever good enough. If Tyler got a B on his report card, his father wanted to know why it wasn't an A. If Tyler won second place in a competition, his father asked why he didn't win first. His father called him weak, soft, a disappointment.

Tyler's mother didn't protect him. She made excuses for his father. "He just wants you to be your best." But the constant criticism crushed Tyler's spirit.

By the time Tyler reached adulthood, he'd internalized his father's voice. Even though he'd moved out and had limited contact with his father, that critical voice lived inside his head now. No matter what Tyler accomplished—and he accomplished a lot—he never felt good enough.

At 32, Tyler was objectively successful. He had a master's degree, a good job, a loving wife. But inside, he felt like a fraud. He worked 70-hour weeks trying to prove himself. He couldn't accept compliments. He was exhausted and depressed.

His wife convinced him to try therapy. Tyler spent a year in traditional therapy exploring his childhood and understanding how his father's treatment had affected him. The therapy helped him understand his patterns, but it didn't change how he felt. He still heard that critical voice. He still felt inadequate.

His therapist suggested EMDR. Tyler had done cognitive work—he understood intellectually that his father was wrong—but the

75

emotional wounds were still there. EMDR might help address those deeper wounds.

The Treatment:

Tyler and his EMDR therapist identified several target memories:

- His father berating him for getting a B in math in fifth grade
- His father calling him weak when Tyler cried after striking out in a baseball game
- His father criticizing his college choice, saying he'd never amount to anything
- His father's dismissive response when Tyler graduated with honors from his master's program

They started with the fifth-grade memory because it seemed to be the earliest formative experience. Tyler's worst image: standing in the kitchen while his father towered over him, yelling. The negative belief: "I'm not good enough." The positive belief: "I'm good enough as I am."

Processing this memory, Tyler felt small and scared again. But as the bilateral stimulation continued, adult Tyler's perspective emerged. He realized his father had impossible standards that no one could meet. He remembered that his teacher had praised that B—it was in advanced math, and Tyler had worked hard for it.

He recognized that his father's criticism said more about his father's issues than about Tyler's worth. His father was a perfectionist who was probably repeating patterns from his own childhood.

As Tyler processed each memory, a pattern became clear: His father's standards were unreasonable. His father's treatment was wrong. Tyler had always been good enough—his father just couldn't see it or wouldn't acknowledge it.

Processing these memories took several months. It wasn't just about the specific incidents. It was about uprooting a belief system that had been built over 18 years of childhood.

The Results:

After eight months of EMDR (about 22 sessions), Tyler's self-perception had transformed.

That critical voice in his head—his father's voice—became quieter. When it did pop up, Tyler could recognize it as his father's issue, not truth about himself.

He stopped working 70-hour weeks. He learned to do his job well without killing himself trying to achieve perfection. He could do "good enough" without feeling like a failure.

He could accept compliments. When his boss praised his work, Tyler could say "thank you" instead of immediately discounting the compliment or finding flaws in his performance.

His depression lifted. The constant anxiety about not measuring up eased. He felt lighter, freer.

"The weirdest thing," Tyler said, "is that I can think about my childhood now without being consumed by it. I can remember my father yelling at me, and I feel bad for that kid I was, but I don't feel destroyed by it. And I can also remember good things from my childhood that I'd kind of forgotten—friends, teachers, moments of happiness. Those memories aren't blocked anymore by the trauma."

Story 4: Patricia - Phobia of Driving After an Accident

The Problem:

Patricia was 28 when she was in a serious car accident. She was driving home from work on a rainy evening. A truck ran a red light and T-boned her car on the driver's side. The impact spun her car around. She ended up with a broken arm, broken ribs, and a concussion.

She recovered physically within three months. But mentally, she was stuck.

Patricia couldn't drive anymore. The first time she tried to get behind the wheel after the accident, she had a full panic attack. Her heart raced, she couldn't breathe, her hands shook so badly she couldn't hold the steering wheel. She had to call her husband to come get her.

She tried a few more times over the next month, always with the same result. Eventually, she gave up. She relied on her husband to drive her everywhere. She took buses when she needed to go places alone. She Ubered to work.

This went on for two years. Patricia's world got smaller. She couldn't be spontaneous. She couldn't help when her kids needed rides. She felt helpless and embarrassed. She'd been an independent person, and now she couldn't do something as basic as drive.

Her doctor recommended EMDR. Patricia had heard of it for PTSD, and she supposed that's what she had—post-traumatic stress about the accident.

The Treatment:

Patricia's EMDR therapist explained that phobias, especially those with a clear traumatic origin, often respond quickly to EMDR. They might need only a handful of sessions.

They identified the target memory: the moment of impact. Patricia's worst image: seeing the truck coming toward her, knowing she was about to be hit and couldn't do anything. The negative belief: "I'm going to die" or "I'm not safe." The positive belief: "I'm safe now" or "I survived."

In the first processing session, Patricia relived the terror of that moment. She shook. She cried. But as they continued with the bilateral stimulation, her brain started making new connections.

She remembered that the accident was over. She'd survived. Her injuries had healed. The truck driver had been at fault, not her— she'd done nothing wrong.

She connected with the fact that she'd driven safely thousands of times before the accident. One bad experience didn't erase all those successful experiences.

She realized that the likelihood of another accident like that was extremely low. She'd been driving for ten years and had one major accident. The odds were in her favor.

Processing took just two sessions to complete the core memory. Then they spent one session working on a "future template"— Patricia imagining herself driving successfully, using bilateral stimulation to reinforce this positive image.

The Results:

After four EMDR sessions spread over four weeks, Patricia was ready to try driving again.

With her therapist's encouragement, she started small. She sat in the driver's seat with the car off, just practicing feeling calm in that position. She used her Safe Place imagery.

Next, she drove around an empty parking lot. Then quiet neighborhood streets. Then busier roads. Finally, highways.

At first, she felt nervous—that's normal. But it wasn't the overwhelming panic from before. She could handle the nervousness. With each successful drive, her confidence grew.

Three months after finishing EMDR, Patricia was driving regularly again. She drove her kids to school. She drove herself to work. She and her husband took a road trip—something they hadn't done since before the accident.

"I still drive carefully," Patricia explained. "I'm more cautious than before the accident. But that's just being smart. The difference is I'm not terrified. I can be in the car without feeling like I'm about to die. EMDR unstuck me."

Story 5: David - Performance Anxiety and Past Humiliation

The Problem:

David was a talented software engineer with a problem: he couldn't present his work. Whenever he had to present to his team or at conferences, he fell apart. His hands shook, his voice trembled, his mind went blank. He'd stumble through presentations, knowing he was doing poorly, which made the anxiety worse.

This was holding back his career. He was brilliant at his actual work, but in tech, you need to be able to present your ideas. His boss had told him directly: "You're great at the technical stuff, but if you can't communicate it, you won't advance."

David had tried everything. Public speaking classes. Beta blockers. Therapy that taught him breathing techniques and positive self-talk. Nothing helped. The panic was too strong.

At 35, David was frustrated. He knew his presentation anxiety was irrational. He could talk to people one-on-one without problems. But put him in front of a group, and he became a mess.

A colleague mentioned EMDR. David was skeptical—how would processing trauma help with presentations?—but he was willing to try anything.

The Treatment:

David's EMDR therapist asked him to trace back his presentation anxiety. When did it start?

David thought about it. He remembered being fine presenting in high school. But in college... he remembered a specific incident. He was 19, giving a presentation in his computer science class. He'd been up late the night before and wasn't fully prepared. He messed up the code demonstration. It didn't work. The professor called him out in front of everyone: "Did you even test this? This is amateur work." Students laughed. David's face burned with humiliation.

That was the first time he'd felt that overwhelming panic during a presentation. And it had been present ever since.

They targeted that college memory. The image: standing at the front of the class, code failing, professor glaring, students laughing. The negative belief: "I'm incompetent." The positive belief: "I'm capable and skilled." SUDS: 8.

As David processed this memory with bilateral stimulation, new perspectives emerged. He remembered that he'd been 19 and sleep-deprived. Everyone makes mistakes, especially when learning. The professor's response had been harsh and unprofessional. Those students probably forgot about it within a day.

He recognized that one failed presentation 16 years ago didn't define his abilities. He'd since completed a computer science degree, gotten a master's, and worked successfully in the field for years.

He realized the professor's harsh words had planted a belief—"I'm incompetent"—that had been running in the background ever since, triggered every time he had to present.

Processing this one memory took just one session. But they also worked on several other related memories:

- A presentation in graduate school where he'd been overly nervous
- His first presentation at his current job, where his anxiety had been visible
- The feedback from his boss about needing to improve his presentation skills

The Results:

After six EMDR sessions over six weeks, David was ready to test his progress. He volunteered to present at the next team meeting.

He prepared thoroughly. Before the presentation, he used the Safe Place technique his therapist had taught him. When he stood up to present, he felt nervous—but it was normal nervousness, not panic. His hands weren't shaking. His mind was clear.

He delivered the presentation successfully. It wasn't perfect—he stumbled over a couple of words—but it was good. Professional. Clear. His team asked questions, which he answered confidently.

After the meeting, his boss pulled him aside: "That was excellent. Whatever you're doing, keep doing it."

David continued presenting regularly. Each time got easier. Six months later, he presented at a major tech conference. He was nervous beforehand, but once he started, he found his groove. The presentation went well. People came up afterward to ask questions and discuss his ideas.

"EMDR didn't make me love presenting," David said. "But it removed the terror. That 19-year-old kid who failed that college presentation isn't controlling 35-year-old me anymore. I can present my work, which means I can advance in my career. That one trauma was holding me back for 16 years, and EMDR cleared it in six weeks."

Story 6: Rita - Complicated Grief After Losing Her Son

The Problem:

Rita's 22-year-old son, Alex, died in a hiking accident. He fell from a cliff. Rita got the call while she was at work. She drove to the hospital, where they told her he hadn't survived.

That was three years ago. Rita knew grief was natural and expected. She knew losing a child was one of the hardest things a person could go through. But her grief wasn't just sadness. It was paralyzing.

She couldn't go through Alex's belongings. His room sat untouched—exactly as he'd left it the morning he went hiking. She couldn't look at photos of him. She couldn't visit his grave. Thinking about him sent her into such intense pain that she had to immediately distract herself.

She felt guilty constantly. Why had she let him go on that hike? Why hadn't she told him to be more careful? Why hadn't she said "I love you" that morning? (She had, actually, but grief made her forget that.)

Rita's husband was worried about her. Her friends were worried. She went to a grief support group, which helped a little. But she wasn't making progress. She was stuck.

Her grief counselor suggested EMDR. Rita didn't understand how EMDR would help with grief—Alex wasn't coming back, so what would processing accomplish? But her counselor explained that Rita's grief was complicated by trauma. The sudden shock of his death, the way she'd learned about it, the visual images her mind had created of the accident—these traumatic elements were preventing her from processing her grief in a healthy way.

The Treatment:

Rita's EMDR therapist was clear: They weren't going to take away her grief or her love for Alex. Grief is appropriate and necessary when you lose someone you love. But they could process the traumatic aspects of his death so Rita could grieve in a healthier way and access her positive memories of him.

They identified several targets:

- The phone call telling her about the accident
- Arriving at the hospital and being told he was dead
- The images her mind had created of him falling (she hadn't witnessed it, but her brain had created vivid, horrible images)
- The guilt about not preventing it

They started with the phone call. Rita's worst image: standing in her office, phone to her ear, hearing "There's been an accident." The negative belief: "I should have protected him." The positive belief: "I loved him and did my best as his mother."

Processing was intensely painful. Rita sobbed through sessions. But gradually, the traumatic charge began to lift.

She remembered that Alex was an experienced hiker who took reasonable precautions. The accident was just that—an accident. It wasn't her fault.

She remembered that she had said "I love you" that morning. She'd told him to be safe. She'd been a good mother who loved her son deeply.

She recognized that her guilt was part of grief's attempt to make sense of something senseless. Parents are supposed to protect their children, so when a child dies, parents often feel they failed—even when there was nothing they could have done differently.

As they processed these traumatic memories, something else became accessible: happy memories of Alex. Rita started being able to think about him without immediately jumping to the accident. She could remember his laugh, his sense of humor, his kindness. She could look at photos without falling apart.

The Results:

After five months of EMDR (about 18 sessions), Rita was in a different place with her grief.

She finally went through Alex's belongings. She kept some things, donated some things, created a memory box with special items. It was sad but not unbearably so.

She could visit his grave. She brought flowers and talked to him, telling him about family news and how much she missed him.

She could look at photos. She created a photo album of her favorite pictures of Alex and put it on her coffee table. Friends could talk about Alex without Rita having to leave the room.

The guilt lessened dramatically. Rita knew intellectually that the accident wasn't her fault, but now she felt that truth. She could think "I was a good mother" without immediately countering it with guilt.

"I still miss Alex every day," Rita said. "I still wish he was here. I still cry sometimes. But I'm not stuck anymore in that moment of trauma. I can remember 22 years of loving my son instead of only remembering the day he died. EMDR helped me find Alex again— not the accident, but Alex himself, the person he was. And I can feel gratitude for the 22 years we had instead of only feeling devastated about the years we lost."

What These Stories Teach Us

These six people had very different problems:

- Combat PTSD
- Sexual assault trauma
- Childhood emotional abuse and low self-esteem
- Accident-related phobia
- Performance anxiety rooted in past humiliation
- Complicated grief

But they all benefited from EMDR because, at the core, they all had the same issue: unprocessed memories that were driving current symptoms.

EMDR helped their brains do what those brains couldn't do on their own—process those memories so they became past events instead of present threats.

Notice that none of these people forgot their past. Marcus still remembers combat. Jennifer still remembers the assault. Rita still remembers losing her son. But those memories transformed from wounds that constantly hurt into scars that mark their history without controlling their present.

That's what EMDR does. It doesn't erase your past. It helps you integrate your past into your life story so you can move forward.

CHAPTER 7: Common Myths About EMDR

People have a lot of questions about EMDR. Some are practical questions about how it works. Others are concerns about what might go wrong. And there are definitely myths floating around. Let's address them all.

"Will EMDR make me relive my trauma?"

Short answer: No.

Longer answer: There's an important difference between *reliving* trauma and *processing* trauma.

Reliving trauma means you're fully immersed in the experience again, feeling like it's happening in the present moment. That's what happens in a flashback, and it's terrifying and retraumatizing.

Processing trauma means you're briefly recalling the memory while maintaining awareness that it's a memory from the past and you're safe in the present. You're thinking about it, yes, and you might feel emotions connected to it, but you're not lost in it.

EMDR is designed to keep you in the processing zone, not the reliving zone. Your therapist keeps you grounded in the present. The bilateral stimulation itself helps maintain that dual awareness—part of your attention is on the memory, and part is on the physical act of following the therapist's hand or feeling the tappers.

If you start to feel like you're reliving rather than processing—if you dissociate or become too overwhelmed—your therapist has techniques to bring you back to the present. This is why the preparation phase is so important. You learn grounding techniques before you start processing, so you have tools if things get too intense.

Gregory's experience:

Gregory was processing a memory of a violent mugging. At one point during the bilateral stimulation, he started to feel like he was back in that moment—he could smell the alley, feel the attacker's hands on him. He started to panic.

His therapist noticed immediately. She stopped the eye movements and said firmly, "Gregory, open your eyes. Look at me. You're in my office. It's 2023. You're safe. The mugging was in 2019. It's over. You survived."

She had Gregory look around the room and name five things he could see. She had him press his feet into the floor. These grounding techniques brought him back to the present.

Then they continued processing, but more carefully, with his therapist checking in more frequently. Gregory successfully processed the memory without getting lost in reliving it.

"Is EMDR hypnosis?"

Short answer: No.

Longer answer: People sometimes think EMDR is hypnosis because both involve focused attention and sometimes seem to produce trance-like states. But they're completely different.

In hypnosis, the goal is often to access a deeper state of consciousness where you're more suggestible. A hypnotherapist might give you suggestions or guide you through visualizations.

In EMDR, you're fully conscious and in control the entire time. You're not in a trance. You're actively processing, and your brain is making its own connections—the therapist isn't implanting ideas or suggestions. You can stop at any time. You can open your eyes and talk. You're fully aware of what's happening.

The bilateral stimulation might make you feel relaxed or a bit zoned out, similar to how you might feel during a long drive. But that's not a hypnotic state. It's just focused attention.

You won't say or do anything you don't want to. You won't reveal secrets you want to keep. You remain in control of yourself and the session.

"Will EMDR erase my memories?"

Short answer: No.

Longer answer: This is a common fear, especially for people processing the death of someone they loved or other significant life events.

EMDR doesn't erase memories. What it does is change how memories are stored in your brain and how your brain reacts to them.

After EMDR, you'll still remember what happened. But the memory will feel different. The overwhelming emotional charge will be gone. The memory will feel more like other old memories— something that happened in the past rather than something that's still happening.

Think of it this way: Before EMDR, the traumatic memory is in bright, painful colors. It's raw and feels immediate. After EMDR, the memory is like an old photograph—still visible, still there, but faded and clearly from the past.

People often worry about this with grief. "If I process my grief, will I forget my loved one?" No. You'll remember them. But the traumatic aspects of their death (the phone call, the hospital, the funeral) won't overshadow all your memories of them. You'll be able to access happy memories again.

Veronica's experience:

Veronica worried that processing her memory of her father's death would somehow diminish her memories of him. She'd been present when he died of cancer after a long illness. The memory of his final days was traumatic—seeing him in pain, watching him deteriorate, being there when he took his last breath.

After EMDR processing those traumatic memories, Veronica found she could think about her father's death without being overwhelmed. But more importantly, she could now access happy memories that had been blocked. She could remember teaching her how to ride a bike, his terrible jokes, family vacations, his pride when she graduated college.

"EMDR didn't make me forget anything," Veronica explained. "It just meant that when I thought about my dad, I didn't automatically jump to those last painful days. I could remember the whole 67 years of his life, not just the final week."

"What if I cry or get really upset during a session?"

Short answer: That's normal and okay.

Longer answer: Processing trauma often involves feeling emotions. You might cry. You might feel angry. You might feel scared. That's expected and appropriate. Your therapist is trained to handle this and won't be alarmed.

Emotions during EMDR are temporary. You might cry for ten minutes during processing, but then the emotion moves through and decreases. That's different from being overwhelmed for hours or days.

Your therapist will check in regularly to make sure you're okay. If emotions become too intense, they'll help you ground and stabilize before continuing.

Remember, you can always stop if you need to. You can take a break, do some grounding, use your Safe Place exercise. You're in control of the pace.

Also know that getting emotional during therapy doesn't mean you're weak or broken. It means you're human and you're processing difficult experiences. Your therapist sees this as normal and even as a sign that the processing is working.

"Can EMDR make things worse?"

Short answer: It's rare, but processing trauma can be uncomfortable.

Longer answer: EMDR is generally very safe when done by a trained therapist. The research shows that adverse effects are uncommon. However, processing trauma isn't always comfortable in the short term.

You might feel worse temporarily. As memories start being processed, you might experience:

- Increased emotions for a day or two after sessions
- More vivid dreams (not necessarily nightmares, but dreams related to what you're processing)
- Memories surfacing that you'd forgotten
- Feeling emotionally raw or tired

These are usually signs that processing is happening, not that something's wrong. Think of it like cleaning out an infected wound—it might hurt at first, but it's necessary for healing.

That said, EMDR shouldn't leave you completely destabilized. If you're having intense symptoms between sessions that you can't manage with your coping skills, tell your therapist. You might need to slow down the pace of processing or spend more time building resources.

There are situations where EMDR should be delayed or approached very carefully:

- Active suicidal ideation
- Severe, unmanaged dissociation
- Ongoing crisis or trauma (like current domestic violence)
- Certain serious mental health conditions that aren't stabilized

A good EMDR therapist will assess your readiness and will only move forward when it's safe to do so.

The bottom line: For most people, when done properly with a trained therapist, EMDR is safe and effective. Short-term discomfort during processing is normal. Being completely overwhelmed and unable to function is not normal—if that happens, tell your therapist.

"Do the eye movements really matter, or is EMDR just exposure therapy?"

Short answer: Researchers are still debating this.

Longer answer: This is actually an ongoing question in the research community. Some studies suggest that the eye movements specifically contribute to EMDR's effectiveness. Other studies suggest that EMDR would work just as well without the eye movements, and that the active ingredient is actually the exposure to the traumatic memory.

Here's what we know for sure:

1. EMDR as a complete protocol (including the eight phases and the bilateral stimulation) is effective. Multiple studies confirm this.
2. EMDR works faster than many other trauma treatments.
3. EMDR doesn't require as much talking about the trauma as exposure therapy does.

What's less clear is exactly why it works. Is it specifically the eye movements? Is it the bilateral stimulation more generally? Is it the structured protocol? Is it some combination?

From a practical standpoint, what matters is that EMDR helps people. Whether the eye movements are essential or just helpful, the overall treatment works.

Most EMDR therapists and researchers believe the eye movements do contribute something. The leading theory is that they activate the same brain processes that happen during REM sleep, when the brain naturally processes memories. But this is still being studied.

If you're the type of person who needs to fully understand the mechanism before trying something, you might find this uncertainty frustrating. But if you're someone who cares more about results than mechanism, the important thing is that EMDR helps, regardless of exactly why.

"Is EMDR scientifically proven?"

Short answer: Yes.

Longer answer: EMDR has been extensively researched. Dozens of controlled studies have examined its effectiveness, particularly for PTSD. The research shows that EMDR is effective and often works faster than other treatments.

Major organizations have recognized EMDR as an evidence-based treatment:

- The World Health Organization (WHO)
- The American Psychiatric Association
- The U.S. Department of Veterans Affairs and Department of Defense
- The International Society for Traumatic Stress Studies
- The U.K.'s National Institute for Health and Care Excellence

That said, EMDR isn't a magic cure-all, and it doesn't work for everyone. Research shows it's highly effective for PTSD and trauma-related conditions. Research on its effectiveness for other conditions (like phobias, depression, anxiety) is more limited but generally positive.

Like any treatment, EMDR works better for some people than others. But the scientific evidence supporting it is strong, especially for trauma.

"How is EMDR different from regular therapy?"

There are several key differences:

Less talking: In traditional talk therapy, you spend a lot of time discussing your problems, your past, your feelings. In EMDR, there's some discussion, but much of the treatment involves the processing itself, which doesn't require much talking.

More structured: EMDR follows a specific eight-phase protocol. Traditional therapy is often more open-ended and follows wherever the conversation goes.

Faster: For trauma, EMDR often works faster than traditional therapy. Where talk therapy for trauma might take years, EMDR might take months.

Different mechanism: Talk therapy often works through insight and understanding—helping you understand why you feel the way you do. EMDR works more directly with how memories are stored, processing them so they stop causing symptoms.

Active processing: In talk therapy, you're primarily talking and thinking. In EMDR, during the processing phases, you're doing bilateral stimulation while your brain actively reprocesses material. It's a more active, less verbal process.

Both approaches have value. Some people need the insight and understanding that talk therapy provides. Some people need the memory processing that EMDR provides. Many people benefit from a combination—using EMDR to process trauma, then doing traditional therapy to work on other life issues.

"Can I do EMDR on myself?"

Short answer: No, not safely or effectively.

Longer answer: You might have seen apps or videos online claiming to provide EMDR or "DIY EMDR." These are not the same as actual EMDR therapy and can be risky.

EMDR isn't just bilateral stimulation. It's an eight-phase treatment protocol that requires:

- Proper assessment and treatment planning
- Adequate preparation and resource building
- Knowing how to target memories appropriately
- Knowing how to handle intense emotions or dissociation
- Knowing when processing is complete
- Following up to ensure the treatment has held

A trained therapist knows how to do all of this. They can keep you safe, help you when you get stuck, and ensure the processing is thorough and effective.

Trying to process trauma on your own can result in:

- Becoming overwhelmed without knowing how to stabilize yourself
- Incomplete processing that leaves you feeling worse
- Accidentally retraumatizing yourself
- Missing related memories that also need processing

Bilateral stimulation by itself (like following a moving dot on an app) isn't harmful, and some people use it for relaxation or stress reduction. But that's not the same as trauma processing.

If you're dealing with trauma, work with a trained EMDR therapist. Don't try to do it yourself.

"What if I can't remember the traumatic event clearly?"

Short answer: That's okay. You don't need perfect recall.

Longer answer: Some people have very clear memories of their trauma. Others have fragmented memories, or their memories are vague and fuzzy. Some people know something traumatic happened but can't remember details.

All of these situations can work with EMDR. You don't need to remember every detail. Your brain has the memory stored somewhere, even if you can't consciously access all of it.

During processing, additional details might emerge. Or they might not. Either way is fine. EMDR can still work.

What you need is:

- A sense of the event or experience
- The emotions connected to it
- The negative belief associated with it
- Where you feel it in your body

Your therapist can work with that, even if you don't have a clear, detailed memory.

Hannah's experience:

Hannah knew she'd been sexually abused as a young child, but her memories were very vague and fragmented. She had images and sensations but not a clear narrative of what happened.

Her EMDR therapist assured her they could still work with this. During processing, some additional details emerged, but the memories never became completely clear—and that was okay. Hannah was able to process the emotions, the body sensations, and the negative beliefs connected to the abuse, even without having complete conscious recall of the events.

The processing worked. Hannah's symptoms decreased. She felt better. Complete memory recall wasn't necessary for healing.

"Will my therapist judge me for what I reveal?"

Short answer: No. Therapists are trained to handle difficult material without judgment.

Longer answer: EMDR therapists hear about trauma regularly. They've heard about abuse, violence, assault, addiction, things people are deeply ashamed of. Nothing you share will shock them or make them think less of you.

Remember, you don't have to go into graphic detail about your trauma. You just need to identify the target memory. Your therapist doesn't need to know every detail—your brain knows the details, and that's what matters for processing.

Also, therapists are bound by confidentiality (with a few specific exceptions like danger to self or others, or abuse of children or vulnerable adults). What you share stays in the therapy room.

If you're concerned about being judged, talk to your therapist about it. A good therapist will reassure you and create a space where you feel safe being vulnerable.

"Can EMDR help with [specific condition]?"

People ask this about all sorts of conditions. Here's a general guide:

EMDR is proven effective for:

- PTSD
- Single-incident trauma
- Complex trauma

EMDR shows promise for (but needs more research):

- Anxiety disorders linked to past experiences
- Depression linked to past experiences
- Phobias with a clear traumatic origin
- Grief complicated by trauma
- Panic disorder
- Performance anxiety

EMDR probably won't help with:

- Conditions with primarily biological/genetic causes (bipolar disorder, schizophrenia, some forms of depression)
- Conditions caused by physical brain injury
- Current, ongoing problems (EMDR works on past memories, not present situations)
- Problems unrelated to past experiences

The key question: Is your condition driven by unprocessed past experiences? If yes, EMDR might help. If no, it probably won't.

When in doubt, consult with an EMDR therapist. They can assess whether EMDR is appropriate for your specific situation.

"How long do the results last?"

Short answer: EMDR's effects are generally long-lasting.

Longer answer: Once a memory is fully processed, it tends to stay processed. Unlike some treatments where you need ongoing maintenance, EMDR's effects usually persist.

Research has followed people months and even years after EMDR treatment. Most people maintain their improvements. The processed memories don't suddenly become traumatic again.

That said, life continues after EMDR. New stressors might arise. You might experience new traumas. But those would be new problems, not a return of the old ones.

Some people return to EMDR later in life if new traumatic events occur or if old memories that weren't previously accessible surface. But this isn't because the original EMDR "wore off." It's because new material needs processing.

"What if EMDR doesn't work for me?"

Not everyone responds to EMDR, just like not everyone responds to any particular treatment. If you've tried EMDR and it's not helping, consider:

Are you with a well-trained therapist? EMDR requires specific training. If your therapist isn't properly trained or experienced, that could affect outcomes.

Have you given it enough time? Some people see rapid results. Others need more sessions. Don't give up after just two or three sessions unless there's a clear problem.

Are you in the right state for processing? If you're in crisis, dealing with current trauma, or lacking basic stability, you might not be ready for EMDR processing yet. You might need more preparation first.

Is your problem actually rooted in past memories? EMDR works on memory-based problems. If your issue has different roots, EMDR might not be the right tool.

Is there something interfering? Ongoing substance use, severe dissociation, or other factors might interfere with processing.

If EMDR truly isn't working after a reasonable trial with a qualified therapist, that's okay. There are other effective treatments for trauma and other mental health issues. EMDR is powerful, but it's not the only option.

Key Take always on Concerns and Myths

EMDR is:

- Safe when done by a trained therapist
- Not hypnosis
- Not going to erase your memories
- Scientifically supported
- Appropriate for many (but not all) mental health conditions

EMDR might involve:

- Temporary discomfort as you process
- Crying or other emotions during sessions
- Feeling tired or emotionally raw after sessions
- Needing multiple sessions to fully resolve symptoms

EMDR won't:

- Make you relive your trauma
- Take away your memories
- Work without a trained therapist
- Fix every problem

If you have concerns or questions, talk to an EMDR therapist. They can address your specific situation and help you decide if EMDR is right for you.

CHAPTER 8: Your EMDR Action Plan

You've read about EMDR. You understand how it works, what it treats, and what to expect. Now comes the important part: actually doing something about it.

This chapter is your practical guide to starting EMDR therapy. We'll cover how to decide if EMDR is right for you, how to find a therapist, how to prepare for your first appointment, and what to do to support your healing process.

Is EMDR Right for You? A Self-Assessment

Before you start searching for therapists, take some time to think about whether EMDR makes sense for your situation.

Ask yourself these questions:

1. Are my current problems connected to past experiences?

Think about the issues you're dealing with. Do they seem to stem from specific events in your past? Do certain situations trigger you in ways that seem connected to old memories?

If yes, EMDR might be helpful.

Examples:

- "I've had anxiety since I was assaulted three years ago."
- "I've been depressed since my mother died."
- "I can't drive since my accident."
- "I've never felt good enough, and I think it goes back to how my parents treated me."

2. Have I tried other treatments that didn't fully work?

If you've done traditional therapy or tried medication and gotten some benefit but still struggle, EMDR might address what those other treatments missed.

3. Am I dealing with trauma or PTSD symptoms?

If you have nightmares, flashbacks, hypervigilance, avoidance, or other PTSD symptoms, EMDR is worth considering. It's one of the most effective treatments for PTSD.

4. Am I stable enough to process trauma?

Honestly assess your current state:

- Are you in crisis right now?
- Are you actively suicidal?
- Are you in a currently dangerous situation?
- Do you have basic coping skills?
- Can you manage difficult emotions with support?

If you're in active crisis or lacking basic stability, you might need other support first before starting EMDR. Talk to a therapist about whether you need preparatory work.

5. Am I willing to feel uncomfortable temporarily?

Processing trauma isn't easy. It might involve temporary increases in emotions or discomfort. Are you willing to go through that short-term discomfort for long-term healing?

6. Can I commit to the process?

EMDR typically requires weekly sessions for several weeks to several months. Can you commit to regular appointments? Do you have the time and resources?

Self-Assessment Scoring:

There's no formal score, but if you answered "yes" to most of these questions, EMDR is worth exploring. If you answered "no" to several, particularly questions 4 and 5, you might want to talk with a therapist about building more stability first or considering other treatment options.

Finding an EMDR Therapist: Your Step-by-Step Guide

Step 1: Use the EMDRIA Directory

Start with the EMDR International Association website: www.emdria.org

Click on "Find a Therapist" and search by your location. You can filter by:

- Training level (trained, certified, consultant)
- Specialties (PTSD, complex trauma, addictions, etc.)
- Whether they offer telehealth
- Languages spoken

Make a list of 5-10 therapists who seem like possibilities.

Step 2: Check Their Websites and Profiles

Most therapists have websites or detailed profiles on therapy directories like Psychology Today. Look for:

- Their credentials and licenses
- Their EMDR training background
- Their areas of expertise
- Their approach to therapy
- Practical information (location, fees, insurance)

Narrow your list to 3-5 therapists who seem like the best fit.

Step 3: Check Insurance Coverage (if applicable)

If you're using insurance, call your insurance company or check their website to see:

- Which therapists on your list are in-network
- What your copay or coinsurance will be
- Whether you need preauthorization for EMDR
- How many sessions are covered

If none of your preferred therapists are in-network, consider:

- Out-of-network benefits (many plans cover some out-of-network care)
- Therapists who offer sliding scale fees
- Whether the investment in paying out-of-pocket is worth it for finding the right therapist

Step 4: Schedule Consultation Calls

Most therapists offer brief phone consultations (usually 10-15 minutes) for free. Call your top 2-3 choices.

During the consultation, ask:

About their background:

- "How long have you been practicing EMDR?"
- "What's your training background in EMDR?"
- "How much of your practice uses EMDR?"
- "Have you worked with clients with [your issue]?"

About the treatment process:

- "How do you structure EMDR therapy?"
- "What does a typical session look like?"
- "About how many sessions do you typically work with someone with [your issue]?"
- "How do you handle it if someone becomes too overwhelmed during processing?"

About practical matters:

- "What are your fees?"
- "Do you take [your insurance]?"
- "Do you offer telehealth, in-person, or both?"
- "What's your availability for appointments?"
- "What's your cancellation policy?"

About fit:

- "What's your approach to therapy?"
- "How do you work with clients who [describe something relevant to you—are skeptical, have complex trauma, etc.]?"

Pay attention not just to their answers but to how the conversation feels. Do they listen? Do they answer your questions thoroughly? Do you feel comfortable talking to them?

Step 5: Make Your Decision

After your consultations, pick the therapist who seems like the best fit. Consider:

- Their experience and training
- Their answers to your questions
- How comfortable you felt talking to them
- Practical factors (cost, location, availability)

Trust your gut. If someone seems great on paper but something feels off, listen to that feeling.

Step 6: Schedule Your First Appointment

Call or email to schedule your intake appointment. Many therapists book out several weeks, so don't be discouraged if you can't get in immediately.

Olivia's therapist search:

Olivia decided to try EMDR for her anxiety, which she believed was connected to childhood experiences with an alcoholic parent.

She searched the EMDRIA directory for therapists in her city. She found 12 names. She checked their websites and narrowed it to four who specialized in complex trauma and anxiety.

She called her insurance company. Two of the four were in-network. She checked those two therapists' websites more carefully. Both looked good.

She scheduled consultation calls with both. The first conversation was fine—the therapist was knowledgeable and professional, but Olivia didn't feel a strong connection. The second conversation felt better. The therapist asked good questions, seemed warm and understanding, and Olivia felt comfortable talking to her.

Olivia scheduled an intake appointment with the second therapist for three weeks later.

Preparing for Your First Appointment

You've found a therapist and scheduled your first session. Here's how to prepare.

Before the appointment:

Complete any intake paperwork. Many therapists send intake forms before the first session. Fill these out completely and honestly. They ask about your history, current symptoms, medications, and what brings you to therapy.

Think about your goals. What do you want to accomplish in therapy? Be as specific as possible.

Vague goal: "I want to feel better." Specific goal: "I want to stop having nightmares about my assault. I want to be able to go on dates without panicking."

Write down your questions. If you have questions about EMDR or therapy in general, write them down so you don't forget to ask.

Gather relevant information. If you have medical records, previous therapy records, or other relevant information, bring copies.

Plan practical details. Know where you're going, how to get there, where to park. Give yourself extra time so you're not stressed and rushed.

What to bring:

- Your insurance card (if applicable)
- Your ID
- Payment method
- A list of current medications
- Your questions and goals
- A notebook if you want to take notes

During the first appointment:

Be honest. Your therapist can only help if they understand what's really going on. You don't have to share everything in the first session, but be truthful about what you do share.

Ask your questions. This is your time. If something confuses you or concerns you, speak up.

Share your goals. Tell your therapist what you're hoping to accomplish.

Discuss your concerns. If you're nervous about EMDR or therapy in general, say so. A good therapist will address your concerns.

Assess the fit. Pay attention to how you feel with this therapist. Do they listen? Do they seem to understand? Do you feel comfortable?

After the first appointment:

Reflect on the experience. Did you feel heard? Did the therapist seem knowledgeable? Did you feel comfortable enough to open up?

Decide whether to continue. You're not locked in after one session. If the fit doesn't feel right, it's okay to try a different therapist.

Do any homework. Your therapist might ask you to do something between sessions—keep a journal, practice a technique, notice patterns. Follow through on this.

Schedule your next appointment. Don't leave without scheduling the next session.

Supporting Your EMDR Journey

EMDR happens in the therapy office, but you can do things outside of sessions to support your healing.

1. Build and maintain your support system.

Processing trauma can be emotionally draining. Make sure you have people you can lean on:

- A partner, family member, or close friend who knows you're in therapy
- Support groups (trauma survivor groups, grief groups, etc.)
- Other supportive relationships in your life

You don't have to share details about your trauma or your therapy if you don't want to. But having people who know you're working through something difficult and who can offer support is valuable.

2. Practice self-care.

Trauma processing takes energy, even if you're not actively "doing" anything during sessions. Take care of your body and mind:

Physical self-care:

- Get enough sleep (7-9 hours for most adults)
- Eat regular, nutritious meals
- Move your body in ways that feel good (walk, swim, dance, stretch)
- Limit alcohol and avoid drugs (they interfere with processing)
- Stay hydrated

Mental/emotional self-care:

- Practice the techniques you learned in therapy (Safe Place, grounding, etc.)
- Do activities you enjoy
- Spend time with people who energize you
- Limit news and social media if they're adding to your stress
- Be patient and kind with yourself

3. Keep a journal.

Your therapist probably asked you to keep track of dreams, memories, or insights that come up between sessions. This serves several purposes:

- It helps you remember things to discuss in your next session
- It helps you track your progress
- It can be cathartic to write things down
- It provides a record of your healing journey

You don't need to write a lot. Even brief notes are helpful:

- "Had a dream about my childhood home. Woke up feeling sad but not panicked."
- "Remembered something about the accident that I'd forgotten."
- "Realized today that I didn't avoid the grocery store even though that's where I usually get anxious."

4. Be patient with the process.

Healing doesn't follow a straight line. You'll have good days and bad days. You might process one memory quickly and another slowly. You might feel worse before you feel better.

Trust that your brain knows how to heal if given the right support. Trust the process, even when it feels slow or uncomfortable.

5. Communicate with your therapist.

Between sessions, if something feels really wrong—if you're in crisis, if you're having thoughts of hurting yourself, if you're more overwhelmed than you can handle—reach out to your therapist. They may have emergency protocols or can help you access crisis support.

Also communicate about the process itself. If sessions feel too intense, say so. If you need to slow down or take a break, speak up. If something your therapist is doing doesn't work for you, tell them. Good therapy is collaborative.

6. Celebrate progress.

Trauma recovery is hard work. Notice and celebrate the improvements, even small ones:

- You had a nightmare but got back to sleep, instead of being awake the rest of the night
- You went to a social event even though you felt anxious
- You had a difficult memory come up but used your coping skills to manage it
- You made it through a processing session even though it was uncomfortable

These are all victories. Acknowledge them.

What to Do After EMDR

Eventually, you'll complete your EMDR treatment. Your target memories will be processed. Your symptoms will have significantly improved. You'll feel ready to end regular therapy.

Follow-up:

Plan follow-up sessions with your therapist—maybe one month after ending, then three months, then six months. These check-ins ensure your progress has held and allow you to address any new material that comes up.

Maintenance:

The EMDR processing doesn't require maintenance—once memories are processed, they stay processed. But maintaining general mental health does require ongoing attention:

- Continue healthy habits (sleep, exercise, social connection)
- Use your coping skills when stressed
- Address new problems early rather than letting them build
- Return to therapy if needed for new issues

Passing it forward:

Many people who've been helped by EMDR want to help others. Consider:

- Sharing your experience (when appropriate) with others who might benefit
- Providing reviews or testimonials for your therapist
- Advocating for mental health treatment and trauma awareness
- Volunteering with organizations that support trauma survivors

Resources

For finding EMDR therapists:

- EMDRIA (EMDR International Association): www.emdria.org
- EMDR Institute: www.emdr.com
- Psychology Today therapist directory: www.psychologytoday.com (filter for EMDR)

For general mental health support:

- National Suicide Prevention Lifeline: 988 (call or text)
- Crisis Text Line: Text HOME to 741741
- SAMHSA National Helpline: 1-800-662-4357

For learning more about EMDR:

- "Getting Past Your Past" by Francine Shapiro (EMDR's creator)
- "Eye Movement Desensitization and Reprocessing (EMDR) Therapy, Third Edition" by Francine Shapiro (clinical textbook, but accessible)
- EMDRIA website has articles and videos explaining EMDR

For trauma education and support:

- "The Body Keeps the Score" by Bessel van der Kolk
- "What Happened to You?" by Bruce Perry and Oprah Winfrey
- National Center for PTSD: www.ptsd.va.gov

Apps that might be helpful:

- PTSD Coach (free, from VA)
- Calm or Headspace (meditation and relaxation)
- DBT Coach (for emotion regulation skills)

Your Action Plan: Next Steps

Let's make this concrete. Here's your action plan:

This week: □ Complete the self-assessment earlier in this chapter □ Decide whether EMDR seems right for you □ If yes, search the EMDRIA directory for therapists in your area □ Make a list of 5-10 potential therapists

Next week: □ Check therapists' websites and profiles □ Verify insurance coverage if applicable □ Narrow your list to your top 3 choices □ Schedule consultation calls

Following week: □ Have consultation calls with 2-3 therapists □ Choose the one who feels like the best fit □ Schedule your first appointment

Before your first appointment: □ Complete intake paperwork □ Write down your goals and questions □ Plan logistics (location, parking, timing) □ Arrange your schedule to allow for appointment and time afterward to process

After your first appointment: □ Assess how it went □ Decide whether to continue with this therapist □ Schedule your next session if moving forward □ Begin any between-session practices

A Final Word

Starting therapy takes courage. Acknowledging that you need help, finding a therapist, showing up for that first appointment—these are all brave acts.

EMDR can be life-changing. It's helped millions of people move past trauma and reclaim their lives. It might help you too.

Your past doesn't have to control your present. The pain you're carrying doesn't have to be permanent. Healing is possible.

Those traumatic memories that have haunted you—the nightmares, the triggers, the constant anxiety—they can be processed and integrated so they no longer run your life. You can think about difficult experiences without being overwhelmed. You can remember without reliving.

You deserve to be free from the pain of unprocessed trauma. You deserve to live fully in the present instead of being stuck in the past. EMDR offers a path toward that freedom.

It won't be easy. Healing never is. But it's worth it.

You've already taken the first step by educating yourself about EMDR. Now take the next step. Find a therapist. Schedule that first appointment. Begin the work.

Your future self—the one who's processed the trauma, who sleeps through the night, who can live without constant fear or anxiety, who feels at peace with the past—is waiting for you on the other side of this work.

Take the step. Start the journey. You've got this.

References

Books

1. Shapiro, F. (2018). Eye Movement Desensitization and Reprocessing (EMDR) Therapy: Basic Principles, Protocols, and Procedures (3rd ed.). New York: The Guilford Press.
2. Shapiro, F. (2012). Getting Past Your Past: Take Control of Your Life with Self-Help Techniques from EMDR Therapy. New York: Rodale Books.
3. van der Kolk, B. (2014). The Body Keeps the Score: Brain, Mind, and Body in the Healing of Trauma. New York: Viking.
4. Levine, P. A. (2010). In an Unspoken Voice: How the Body Releases Trauma and Restores Goodness. Berkeley, CA: North Atlantic Books.
5. Herman, J. L. (2015). Trauma and Recovery: The Aftermath of Violence—From Domestic Abuse to Political Terror (3rd ed.). New York: Basic Books.
6. Rothschild, B. (2000). The Body Remembers: The Psychophysiology of Trauma and Trauma Treatment. New York: W.W. Norton & Company.
7. Leeds, A. M. (2009). A Guide to the Standard EMDR Therapy Protocols for Clinicians, Supervisors, and Consultants. New York: Springer Publishing.

Journal Articles and Research Studies

8. Shapiro, F. (1989). Eye movement desensitization: A new treatment for post-traumatic stress disorder. Journal of Behavior Therapy and Experimental Psychiatry, 20(3), 211-217.
9. Bisson, J. I., Roberts, N. P., Andrew, M., Cooper, R., & Lewis, C. (2013). Psychological therapies for chronic post-traumatic stress disorder (PTSD) in adults. Cochrane Database of Systematic Reviews, 12, CD003388.

10. Wilson, S. A., Becker, L. A., & Tinker, R. H. (1995). Eye movement desensitization and reprocessing (EMDR) treatment for psychologically traumatized individuals. Journal of Consulting and Clinical Psychology, 63(6), 928-937.
11. Lee, C. W., & Cuijpers, P. (2013). A meta-analysis of the contribution of eye movements in processing emotional memories. Journal of Behavior Therapy and Experimental Psychiatry, 44(2), 231-239.
12. Carlson, J. G., Chemtob, C. M., Rusnak, K., Hedlund, N. L., & Muraoka, M. Y. (1998). Eye movement desensitization and reprocessing (EMDR) treatment for combat-related posttraumatic stress disorder. Journal of Traumatic Stress, 11(1), 3-24.
13. Marcus, S. V., Marquis, P., & Sakai, C. (1997). Controlled study of treatment of PTSD using EMDR in an HMO setting. Psychotherapy: Theory, Research, Practice, Training, 34(3), 307-315.
14. Rothbaum, B. O. (1997). A controlled study of eye movement desensitization and reprocessing in the treatment of posttraumatic stress disordered sexual assault victims. Bulletin of the Menninger Clinic, 61(3), 317-334.
15. De Jongh, A., Ten Broeke, E., & Renssen, M. R. (1999). Treatment of specific phobias with eye movement desensitization and reprocessing (EMDR): Protocol, empirical status, and conceptual issues. Journal of Anxiety Disorders, 13(1-2), 69-85.
16. Ironson, G., Freund, B., Strauss, J. L., & Williams, J. (2002). Comparison of two treatments for traumatic stress: A community-based study of EMDR and prolonged exposure. Journal of Clinical Psychology, 58(1), 113-128.
17. Power, K., McGoldrick, T., Brown, K., Buchanan, R., Sharp, D., Swanson, V., & Karatzias, A. (2002). A controlled comparison of eye movement desensitization and reprocessing versus exposure plus cognitive restructuring versus waiting list in the treatment of post-traumatic stress disorder. Clinical Psychology & Psychotherapy, 9(5), 299-318.

Clinical Guidelines and Reports

18. World Health Organization. (2013). Guidelines for the Management of Conditions Specifically Related to Stress. Geneva: WHO.
19. American Psychiatric Association. (2004). Practice Guideline for the Treatment of Patients with Acute Stress Disorder and Posttraumatic Stress Disorder. Arlington, VA: American Psychiatric Publishing.
20. Department of Veterans Affairs & Department of Defense. (2017). VA/DoD Clinical Practice Guideline for the Management of Posttraumatic Stress Disorder and Acute Stress Disorder (Version 3.0). Washington, DC: Authors.
21. National Institute for Health and Care Excellence. (2018). Post-Traumatic Stress Disorder: NICE Guideline [NG116]. London: NICE.
22. International Society for Traumatic Stress Studies. (2018). Posttraumatic Stress Disorder Prevention and Treatment Guidelines: Methodology and Recommendations. Oakbrook Terrace, IL: Author.

Book Chapters and Edited Volumes

23. Shapiro, F., & Maxfield, L. (2002). Eye movement desensitization and reprocessing (EMDR): Information processing in the treatment of trauma. Journal of Clinical Psychology, 58(8), 933-946.
24. Solomon, R. M., & Shapiro, F. (2008). EMDR and the adaptive information processing model: Potential mechanisms of change. Journal of EMDR Practice and Research, 2(4), 315-325.
25. Hase, M., Balmaceda, U. M., Ostacoli, L., Liebermann, P., & Hofmann, A. (2017). The AIP model of EMDR therapy and pathogenic memories. Frontiers in Psychology, 8, 1578.

The information in this book is drawn from extensive research, clinical studies, and established EMDR protocols. The following references represent key sources in the field of EMDR therapy and trauma treatment. Readers interested in learning more are encouraged to explore these resources and consult with qualified mental health professionals.

www.ingramcontent.com/pod-product-compliance
Lightning Source LLC
LaVergne TN
LVHW021518080426
835509LV00018B/2559